ROBERT GOBER

ΔΕΣΤΕ

DESTE Foundation for Contemporary Art

ROBERT GOBER

2000 WORDS

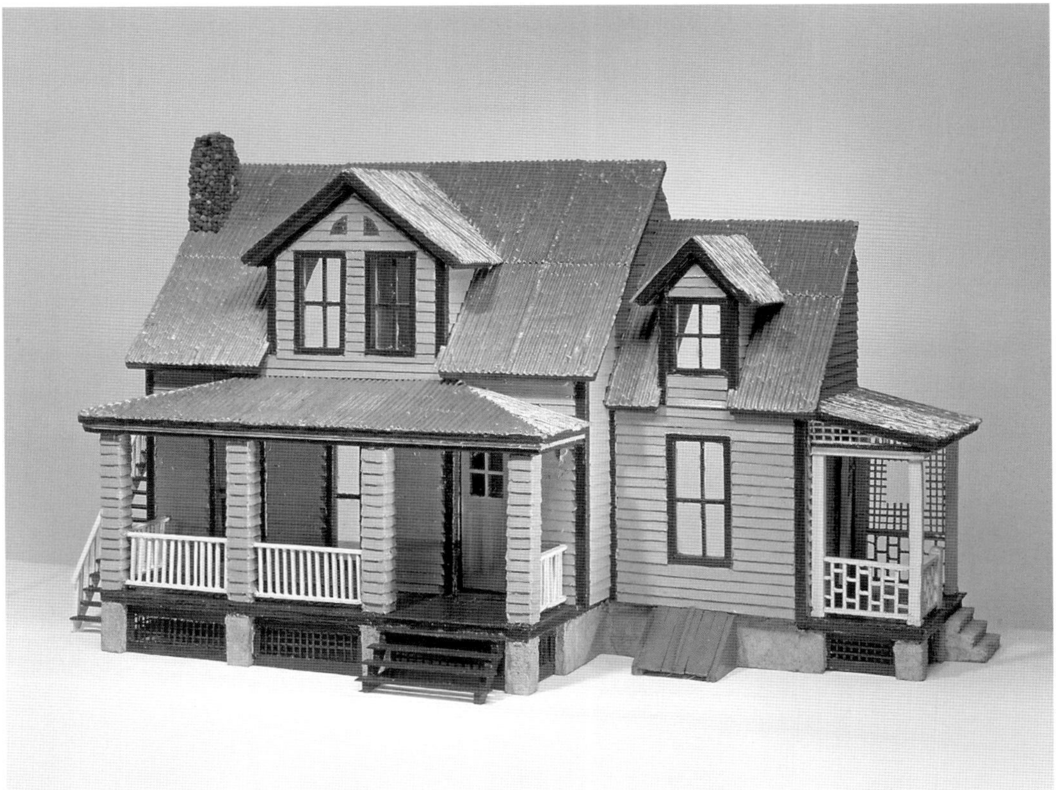

BEHIND THE SCENES

Johanna Burton

In the sizeable literature devoted to Robert Gober's nearly thirty-year career, one regularly encounters two arguments. The first asserts that there is something deeply—endemically—mysterious about the objects and environments Gober creates; that inherent to them is a kind of unknowability, a deeply held, covert kernel at each one's core. (This position is asserted most poetically by the critic Hal Foster, who writes of Gober, "this is the work of his work: *to sustain enigma*."[1]) The second overarching claim hewing to the artist's œuvre is that it proceeds by way of re-presenting nearly universal images; in other words, while each viewer's references key uniquely to Gober's works, these are nonetheless familiar to everyone, immediately recognizable within a spectrum of shared human experience. As curator Theodora Vischer writes—referring both to Gober's expansive œuvre and to our almost primal reactions to it—this nexus of "personal history and collective, common property" is located firmly within "ordinary domestic life." Indeed, she asserts, "That is where it all begins."[2]

What would seem to be a deep incongruity—Gober's work posited as both obtuse *and* transparent; as forthright *and* undercover—offers instead an unexpectedly acute portrait of the artist's practice, and reception, as it has evolved over years and across mediums. For efforts to account for such a persistent, internal incompatibility have led, naturally enough, to considering Gober through the lens of Surrealism (ordinary objects made strange through violent encounters, à la the umbrella and the sewing machine); the uncanny (revealing the eerie underbelly of the utterly familiar); and the abject (traumatic conduit to the precarious, fractured body). Yet however illuminating readings of Gober's work within these theoretical contexts might prove, something is inevitably lost in such an immediate move away from the objects themselves to, instead, all they conjure.

Along these lines, it is interesting that Gober once explained, "I always try to get people to focus less, or at least not first, on finding 'meaning' or a 'theme' in the work, but to focus on what it is exactly, what is it physically made of and how it is made. A lot of times metaphors are almost embedded in the medium."[3] The comment is seemingly straightforward, but Gober's words here are, on closer consideration, as subtly dualistic as his work. While asking viewers to look carefully at objects, to consider their physical beings *first*, the artist nevertheless recognizes something inherent, though often under-recognized, in base materiality itself. "Metaphors are almost embedded in the medium," he says. In this way Gober suggests not only that matter itself is always already suggestive of other matter—*metaphor* is, we know, defined as a "carrying over or across"—but also that the objects we encounter are hardly empty vessels waiting to be filled with our content, however much we, as viewers, bring associations, memories, and vocabulary to them. In fact, and quite to the contrary, Gober implies, these objects meet us halfway, with lives of their own, already full of significance, even while still motivated toward assuming additional, even alternative, implications.

To say so is only to repeat something the artist has noted in others' work. Writing in 2004 for an issue of *Artforum* devoted to looking back at Minimalism, Gober reflected on his arrival to New York City in 1976 and his initial experience of artworks by Carl Andre and Donald Judd. Titled "Behind the Seams," Gober's short text argues that, how ever foundational these two artists, their practices constitute two distinct sides of Minimalism's coin. Moreover, without positing one's approach as more valuable than the other's, Gober describes Andre and Judd as fundamentally at odds—even as they produced the necessary conditions for the vibrant artistic project of Minimalism, at least as Gober chose to inherit it. As Gober argues, Andre's work "is what it is. If you pick up a metal plate or a timber and turn it over and look underneath, its essence always remains the same." On the other hand, Judd's works "appear to be what they are, but actually there is always a bit of old-fashioned stagecraft involved. . . . Judd's sculptures announce themselves as paradigms of clarity and forthrightness, yet achieve this goal through formal deception."[4]

Such "formal deception" in Judd's work is, ultimately, also somewhat banal—Gober points to the mechanism by which the older artist's wall works are mounted on internal brackets as the concrete example of his sleight of hand—and impressive showmanship, the artist suggests, is only as good as what's behind the scenes, making things possible. This can happen in (at least) two ways: via utter transparency (Andre's metal plate "is what it is," no matter from what angle you observe it) or by way of dramatic staging (Judd's seemingly straightforward geometry as literally propped up from within). And, taking up these tenets in order to arrive at a broader formulation about sculpture, Gober says that the medium "is always, I believe, a way of expressing impressions about your life on earth." Here, he does not explicitly address what Andre's practice reveals about his experience of the world, probably because it's all, well, there on the surface. But of Judd, Gober says, quite provocatively for his own practice: "There is a masculine bluff about these works that I find endearing, emotionally complex, and perhaps in their duplicity quintessentially American."[5]

At first blush, Minimalism (no matter the underlying impulse) would seem the utter reverse of Gober's work—the former's famed aversion to narrative and representation given hyperbolic attention by the latter. Yet, as with all such ostensible opposites, the differential is slim indeed, and one need only gently prod Judd's aluminum boxes to make them into Gober's slabs of oversized butter; and squint at Andre's regimented tiles to imagine them as the backsplash of Gober's obsessively replicated sinks (themselves tipping ever so easily over into becoming torsos and gravestones). To suggest as much isn't to posit Gober's work as a direct response to Minimalism, but, rather, a return to his own prompt that we look closely at what's in front of us—not only with an eye to how the object is made and what it's made of, but also to how meanings flow between materials and, by extension, across histories.

So, when one looks at a work by Gober, what does one see? One is tempted to say "a leg," or "a stack of newspapers," or "a sink," depending on the work in question. But, of course, this list—and a much longer one, made up of repeating and singular icons within the artist's œuvre—names what's represented in front of you, instead of what's actually there. Listing the materials doesn't fare us much better. It matters, of course, that the fifty-odd sinks the artist produced between 1984 and 1986 were mostly made by way of a multi-step, time-intensive manual system in which Gober applied plaster to wire mesh, built up its form, then sanded, dried, and painted it so it nearly passed as the real thing.[6] However, understanding something of the process by which these objects are made is revealing, but not revelatory. Like Judd's "stagecraft," Gober's is less magic than muscle power and manipulation. Looking at a work by Gober, then, lies somewhere between: what we see is one object in the act of representing another object. The space between the former and the latter is what we (myself included, in this very essay) try so hard, yet fail, to name.

The philosopher Cora Diamond has written

an essay that seems especially pertinent in this regard, dedicated to the "experience of the mind's not being able to encompass something which it encounters."[7] Providing examples by which to consider this phenomenon, Diamond takes up in particular considerations of the concept of death and the psychic life of animals as two prime "experiences in which we take something in reality to be resistant to our thinking it, or possibly to be painful in its inexplicability, difficult in that way, or perhaps awesome and astonishing in its inexplicability."[8] Death and animals, that is to say, fall outside the purview of language, leaving humans to grapple with them clumsily or to ignore them altogether.

In this vein, Gober, of course, is often discussed for his overt attention, both as an artist and an activist, to the AIDS epidemic, a crisis of massive proportions that was not recognized by the American government until some 37,000 people had been diagnosed and 21,000 had died.[9] His early sink works are often read as stand-ins for the body, and as traumatic reminders that one could not cleanse oneself or one's loved ones of the virus. Such readings came to mind again when, years later, after the terrorist attacks of 9/11, Gober produced a series of photolithographs replicating newspaper reports in the immediate wake of the events. Over the top of images and narratives detailing the carnage and confusion of that day, Gober placed delicate renderings, in pastel and graphite, of fragmented bodies—couples embracing, huddled together naked, in comfort or coitus.

These two moments in Gober's work—and life—evince strong reactions in most viewers, keyed as they are to extreme contexts, and to particular moments in history. But these examples only make clear that the artist asks questions about the fine line between life and death, subjecthood and subjection, pleasure and pain, throughout his œuvre. His early dollhouses, which Gober at first didn't consider art, disclosed something of the strange constructions we take for granted as armatures for family, and, later, social life. By literally or figuratively warping the expected contours of things—in sculptures and installations approximating cribs, beds, and wallpapered rooms, for instance—Gober destabilizes ostensibly shared conventions, laying bare their ideological fray. What's more, he quietly places us at a remove from our own relationships to things. For a moment we struggle to articulate the fundamental aspects of our own formation and how we arrived at them.

The significance of such an endeavor for Gober's work is perhaps best underscored by a book project the artist presented alongside his United States pavilion as part of the 2001 Venice Biennale, for which he employed recently rediscovered photographs taken in 1978 during a car trip from Manhattan to Jones Beach with a group of friends. Along the way, Gober had snapped a series of pictures which formed the loosest narrative tableau: bumper-to-bumper traffic, city buildings as seen from a bridge, the eventual escape to nearby nature, with its own crammed parking lot, and, nearby, horizontal bodies lounging on the sand. Put in a drawer and only found decades later, however, these pictures existed solely on a beat-up contact sheet. And so Gober proceeded to rephotograph them, and to make another sequence of pictures which would eventually layer onto the previous images—more precisely, the new pictures were set squarely in the middle of the older images, with the whole photographed again, ultimately comprising, new single images. These strange pictures, in which information is doubled but only by way of creating a literal blind spot, were titled by the time period their production traversed, *1978–2000*. The newest pictures were also taken on Long Island, this time near the artist's studio, and largely document the formidable debris accruing there—chip bags, tires, and slabs of Styrofoam—while two more striking images feature clippings from late 1990s articles in the *New York Times*. One article details the brutal killing of a man thought to be gay; and another, a letter to the editor, uses twisting logic to make the case that homophobia is legitimate when understood within the context of and principles laid out by organized religion. In Gober's photographs the articles are cradled, one in the palm of a hand, the other rested between a pair of jeaned legs, forming a triangle on the sand. One assumes the legs are Gober's but, interestingly, and perhaps tellingly, they are prosthetics constructed for the shoot.[10] *1978–2000* tells a kind of abstract story, using an urban landscape to almost diagram the ways in which we make distinctions: between nature and culture; the valuable and the worthless; the moral and the perverse.

In the Venice book project, in other words, Gober literally exposes his showmanship and, with it, the American duplicity he admired, but has efficiently queered, in Judd. Gober's project, however, is anything but genealogical. Judd's works are, like anything Gober reacts to, entities in space, with their own pasts, presents, and futures. Indeed, complicating the very notion of "influence," Gober points to the ways in which one's subjectivity, to say nothing of one's art, is shaped by everything around it. "As if," he says, "the gutter, misunderstandings, memories, sex, dreams, and books matter less than forebears do. After all, in terms of influences, it is as much the guy who mugged me on 10th Street, or my beloved dog who passed away much too early, as it was Giotto or Diane Arbus."[11] In saying so, Gober gives it all away, and yet, once again, we are no closer to articulating what "it" is.

1 Hal Foster, "An Art of Missing Parts," *October* 92 (Spring 2000): 131.
2 Theodora Vischer, "An Attempt at an Introduction," *Robert Gober: Sculptures and Installations 1979–2007* (Basel: Schaulager; Göttingen: Steidl, 2007), 12–13.
3 "Bob Gober Talks with Daphne Fitzpatrick and Allison Smith," *Interview Magazine* (June 2001): 89.
4 Robert Gober, "Behind the Seams," *Artforum* 42 (Summer 2004): 210.
5 Ibid.
6 See, among other texts by the conservator Christian Scheidemann, "Robert Gober's Painted Sculpture," in Ann Temkin, ed., *Robert Gober: The Heart Is Not a Metaphor* (New York: Museum of Modern Art, 2014), 246–54. Scheidemann details the rendering of a number of Gober's works and emphasizes the strange status of his objects, as both sculptures and dimensional paintings.
7 Cora Diamond, "The Difficulty of Reality and the Difficulty of Philosophy," in Stanley Cavell et al., *Philosophy and Animal Life* (New York: Columbia University Press, 2008), 43–90.
8 Ibid., 46.
9 A "rare cancer" affecting gay males was announced by the CDC in 1981. President Reagan did not say "AIDS" until 1987. See Lawrence K. Altman, "Rare Cancer Seen in 41 Homosexuals," *The New York Times*, July 3, 1981, A20, reproduced in *The Heart Is Not a Metaphor*, 127. Estimates of deaths and diagnoses are understood to be inaccurate and low due to the many instances in which individuals or their families, in efforts to maintain privacy or avoid being ostracized, reported causes other than AIDS.
10 See James Rondeau, "Excavation: Robert Gober's New Work in Venice," in James Rondeau and Olga M. Viso, *Robert Gober: The United States Pavilion, 49th Venice Biennale* (Chicago: The Art Institute of Chicago; Washington, D.C.: Hirshhorn Museum and Sculpture Garden, Smithsonian Institution, 2001). Gober comments that he included the piece legitimizing hate speech in part because it allowed him to "both object to and protect the right to express this piece of thinking" (ibid., 40).
11 Robert Gober, "Introduction," in Cynthia Burlingham and Robert Gober, eds., *Heat Waves in a Swamp: The Paintings of Charles Burchfield* (Los Angeles: Hammer Museum; New York: DelMonico Books/Prestel, 2009), 8.

WORKS

Dollhouse 4, 1978

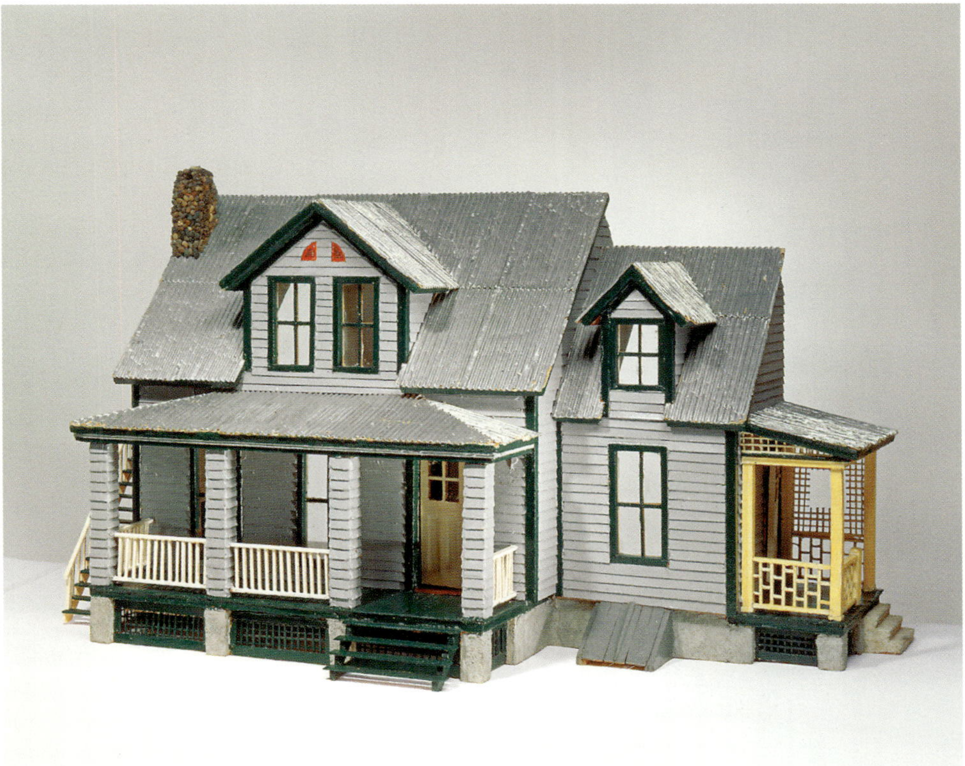

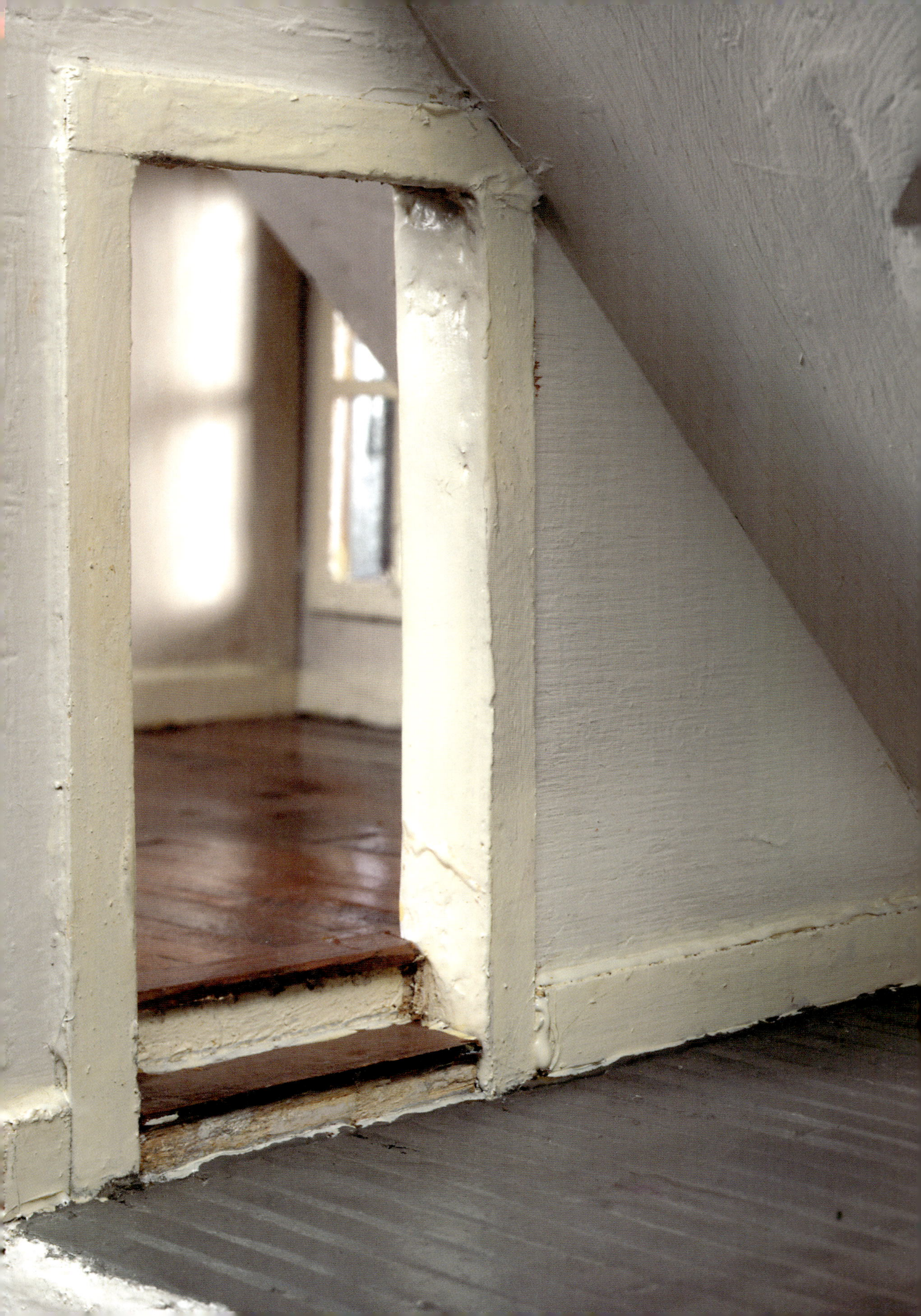

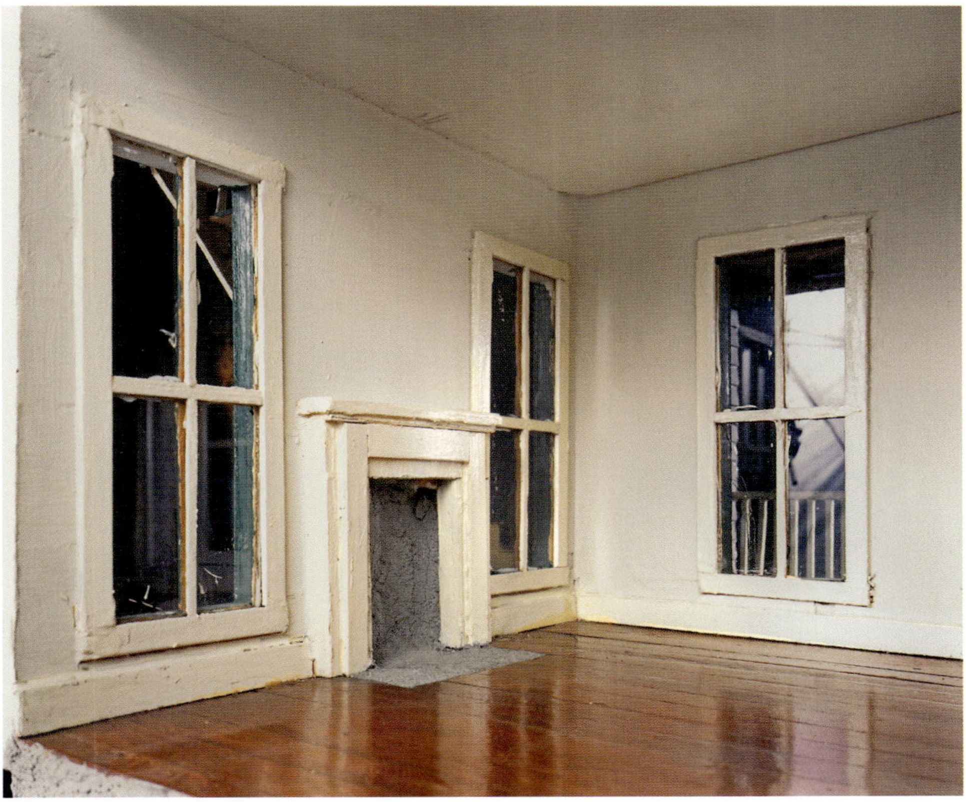

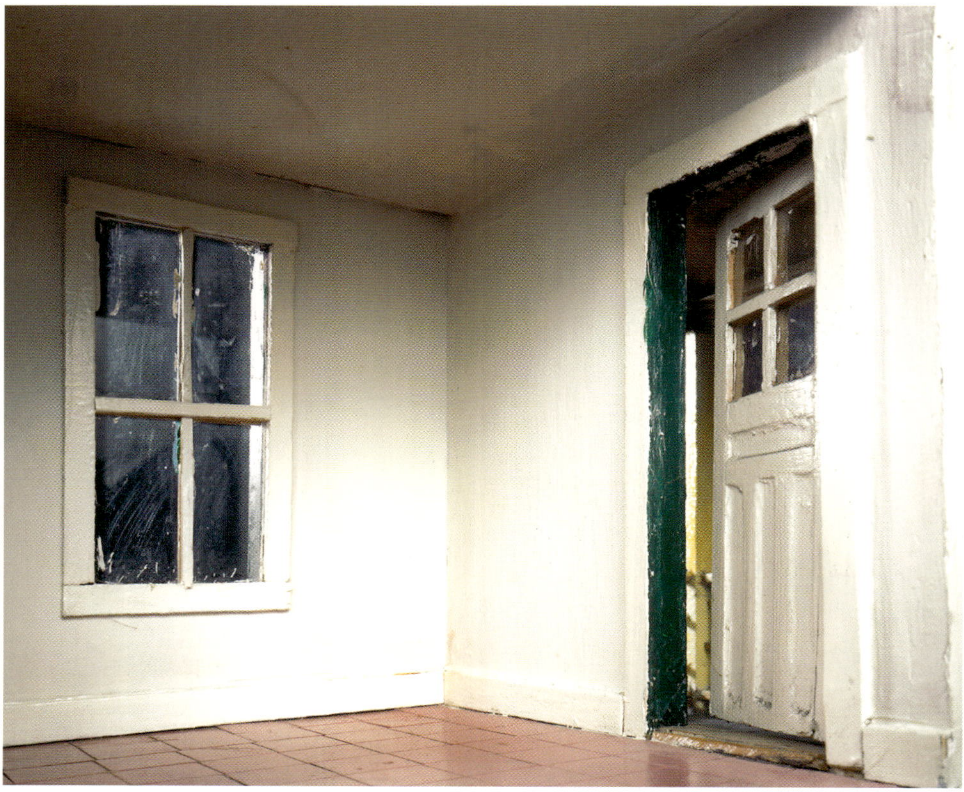

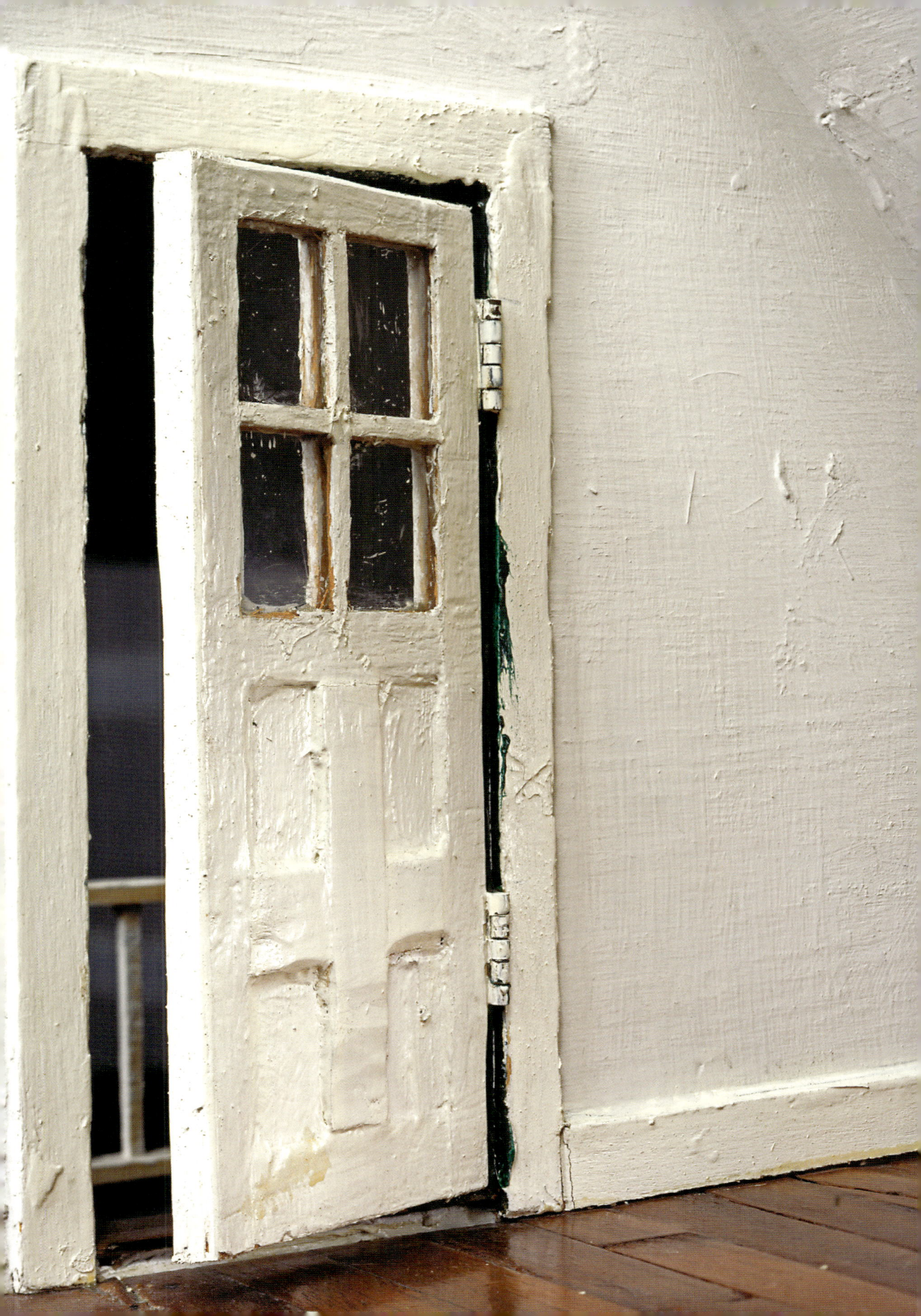

1978-2000, 1978-2000

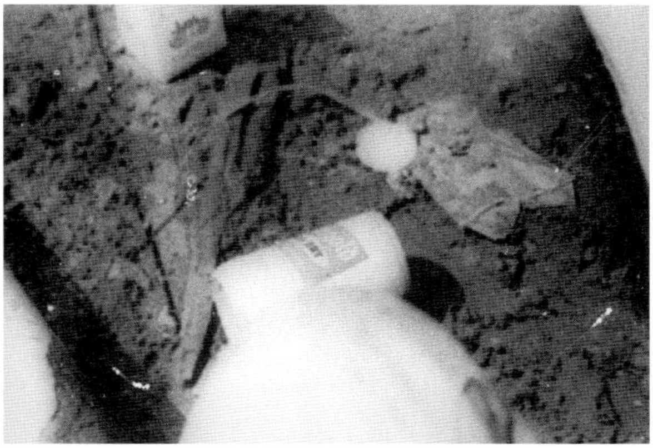

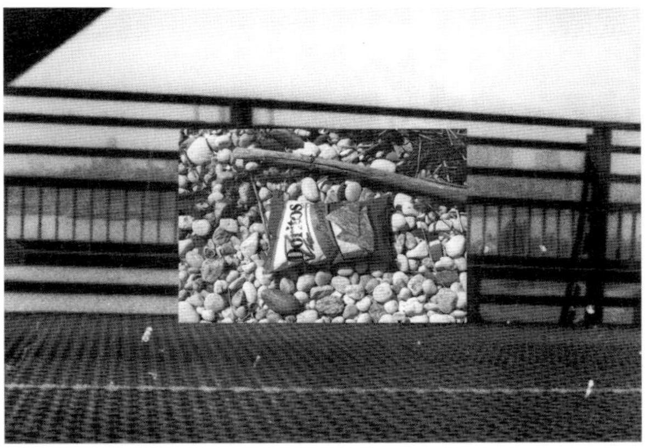

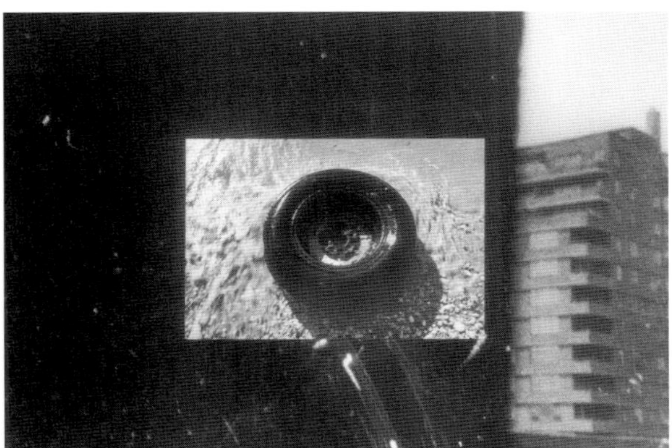

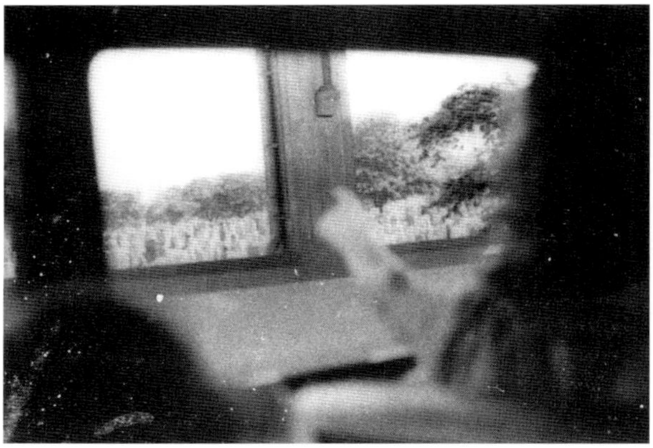

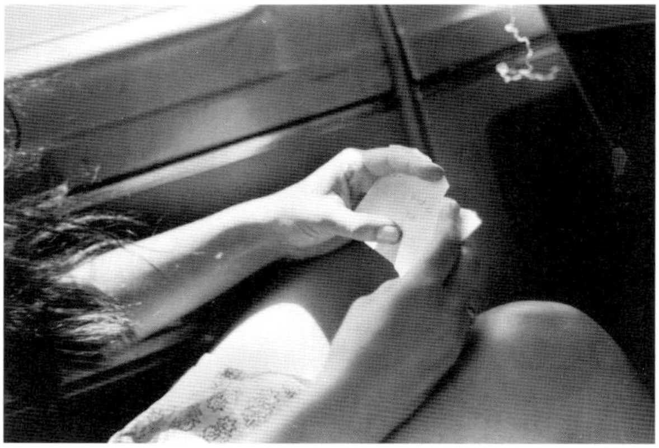

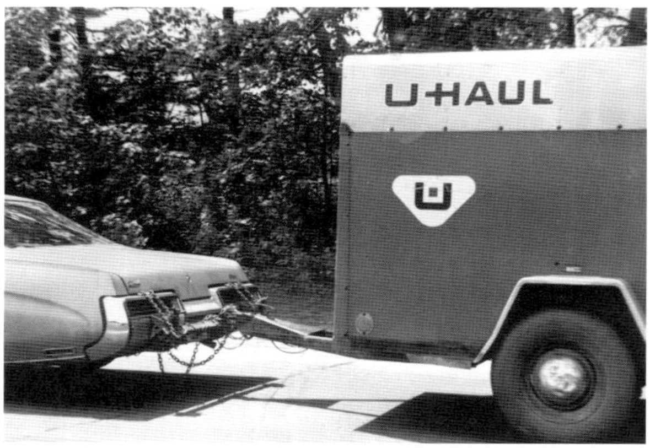
U-HAUL

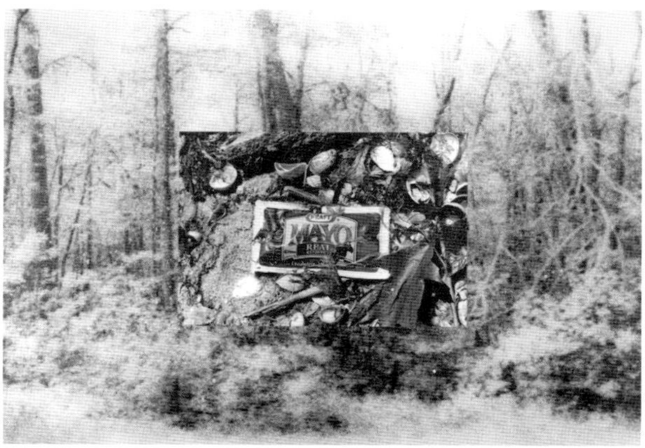

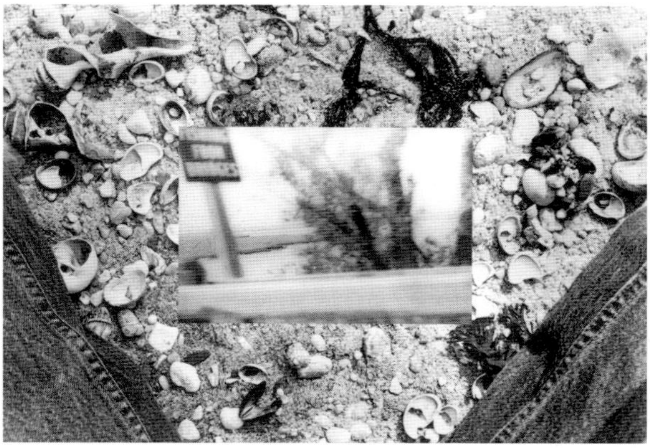

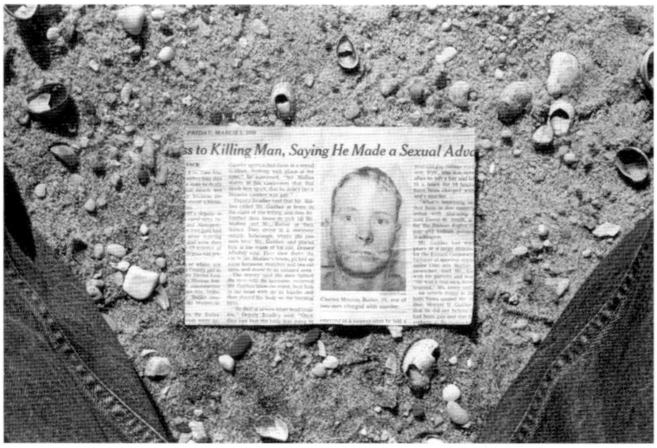
to Killing Man, Saying He Made a Sexual

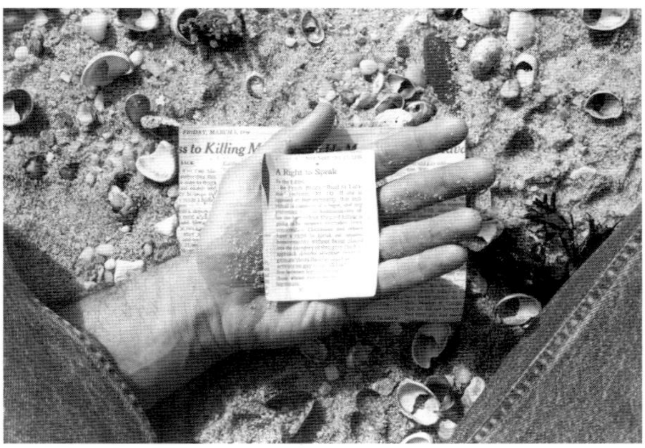
A Right to Speak

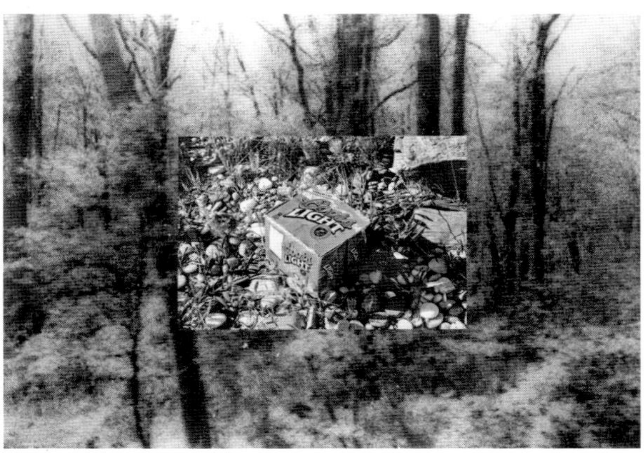
LIGHT

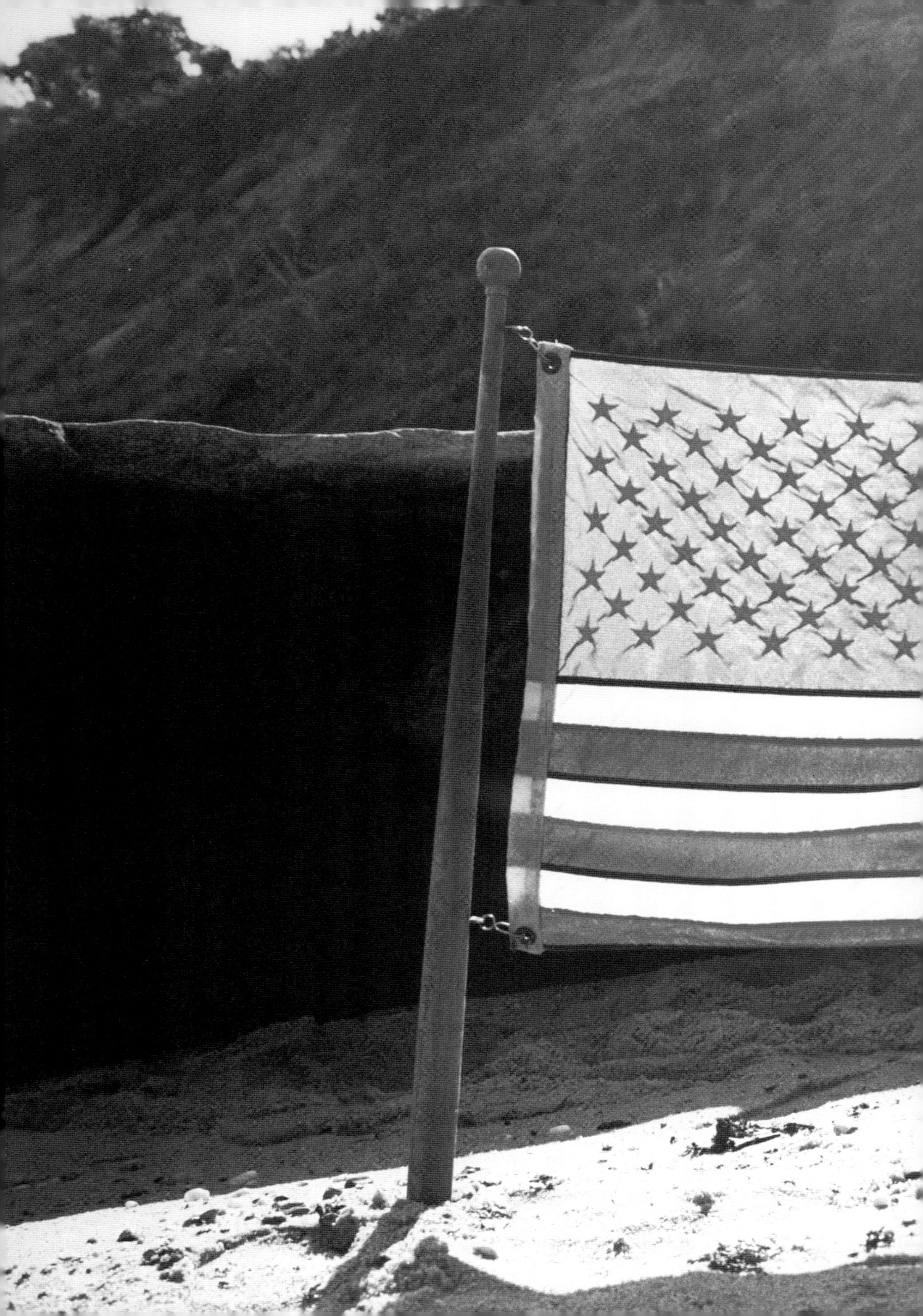

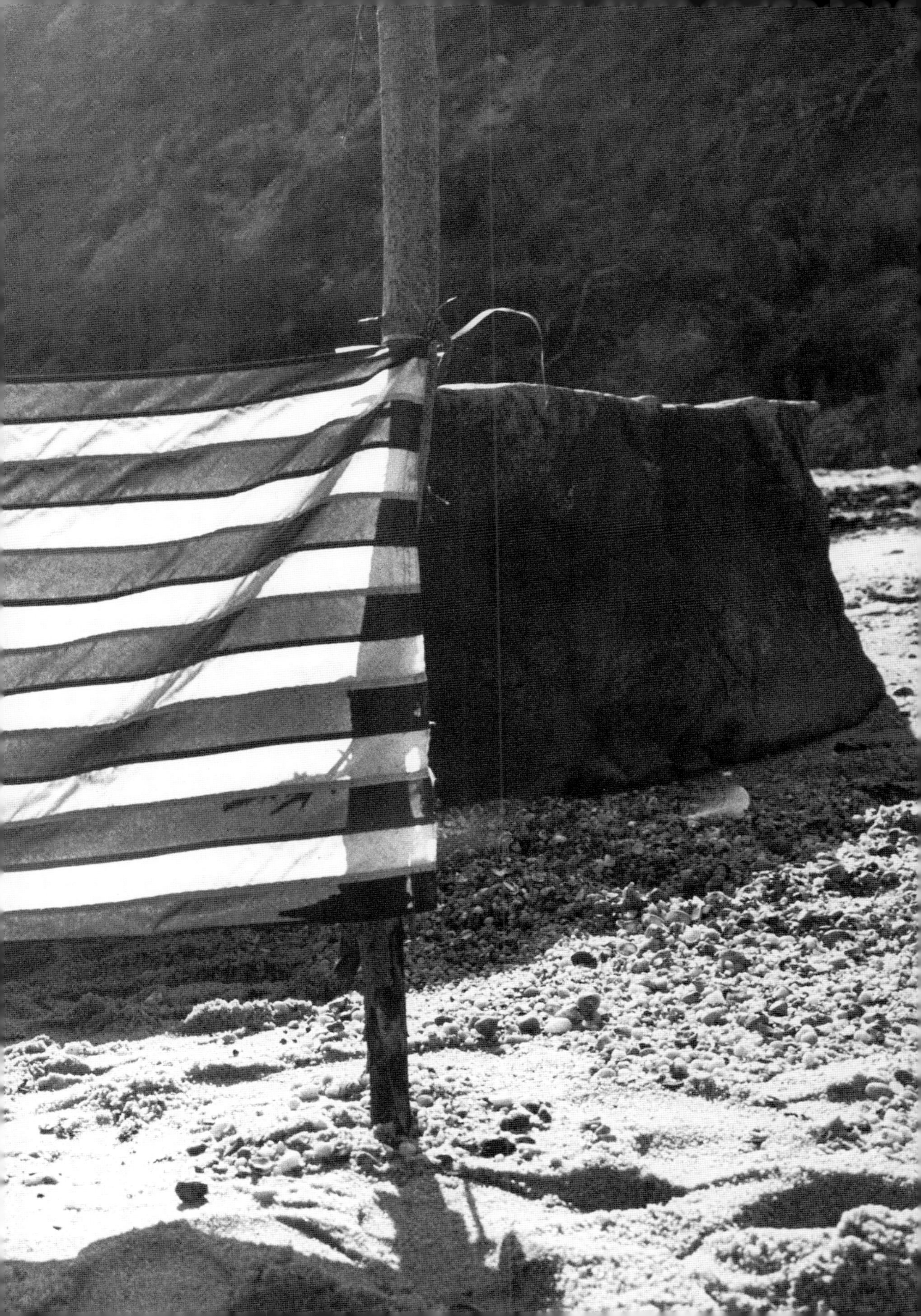

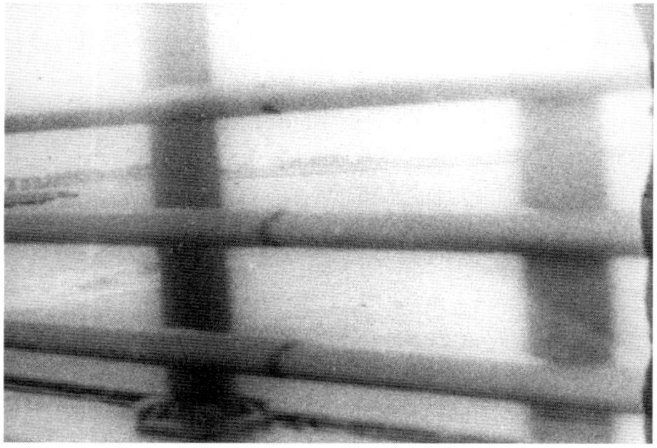

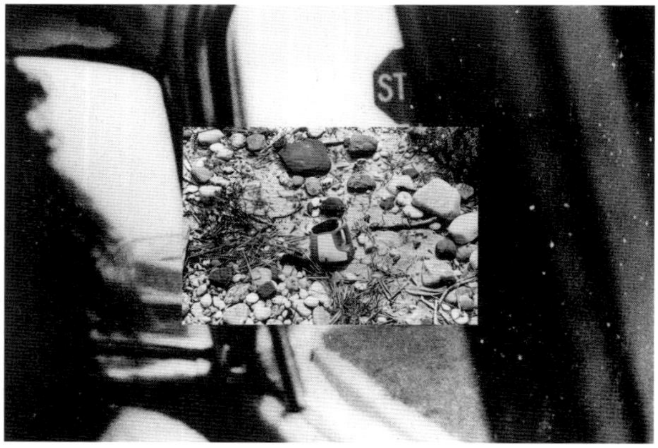
ST

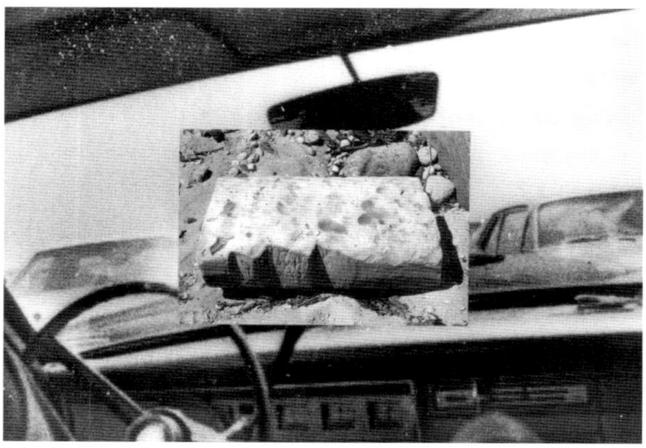

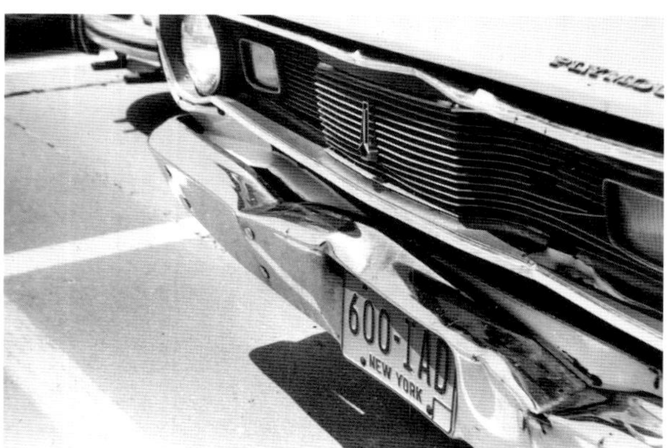
600-IAD
NEW YORK

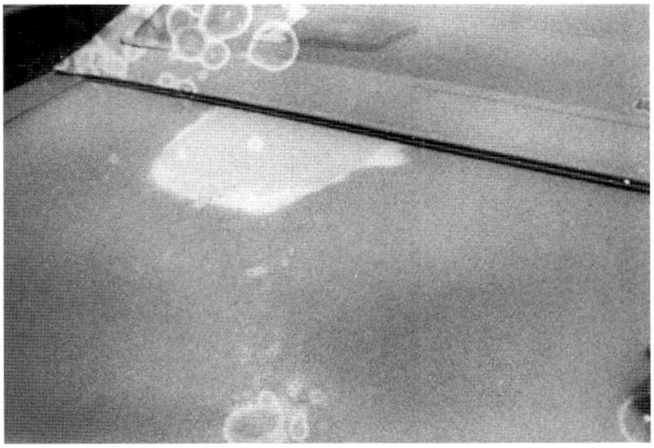

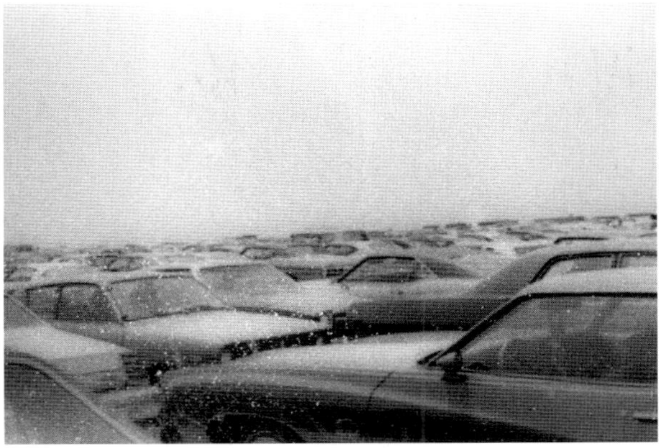

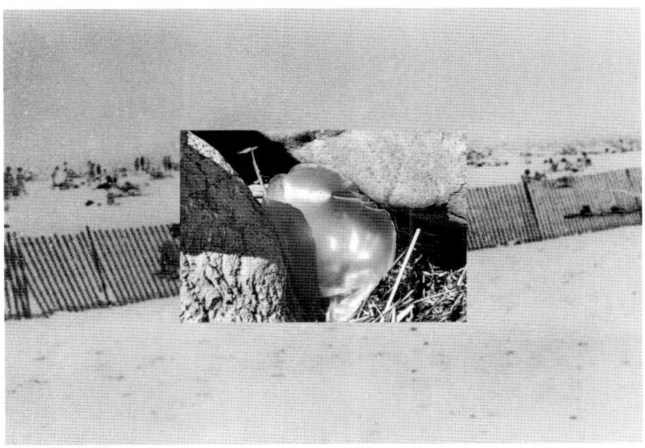

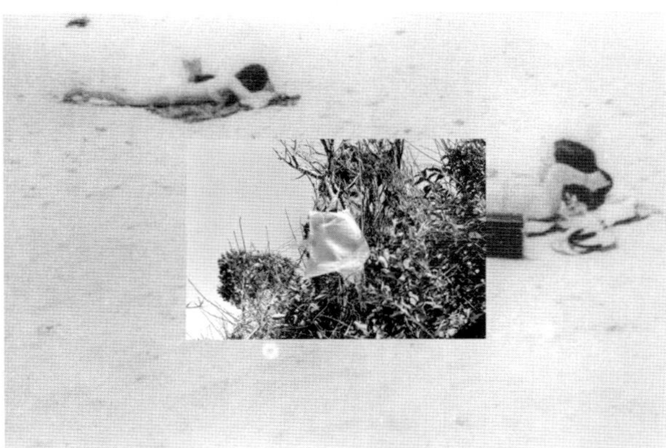

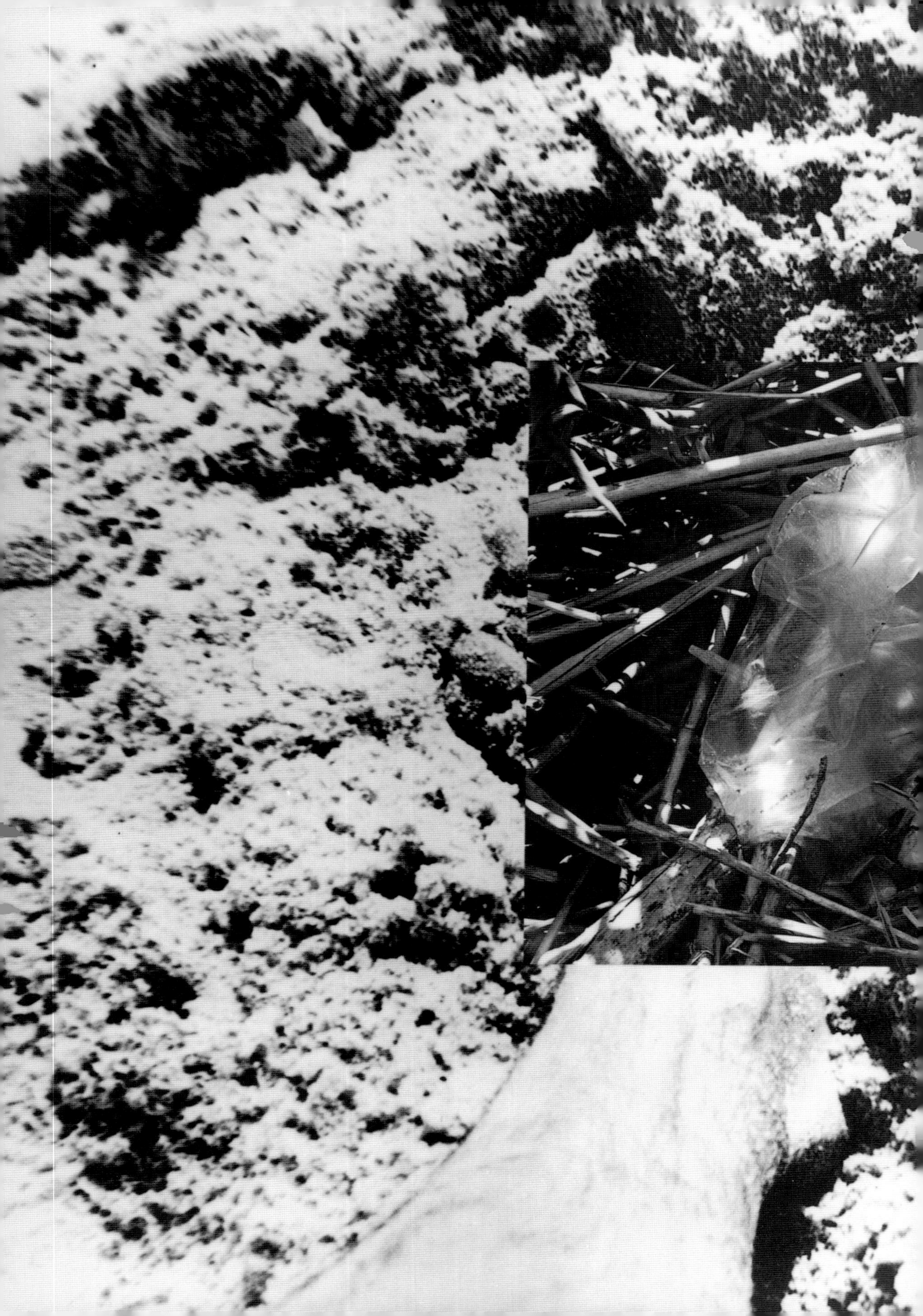

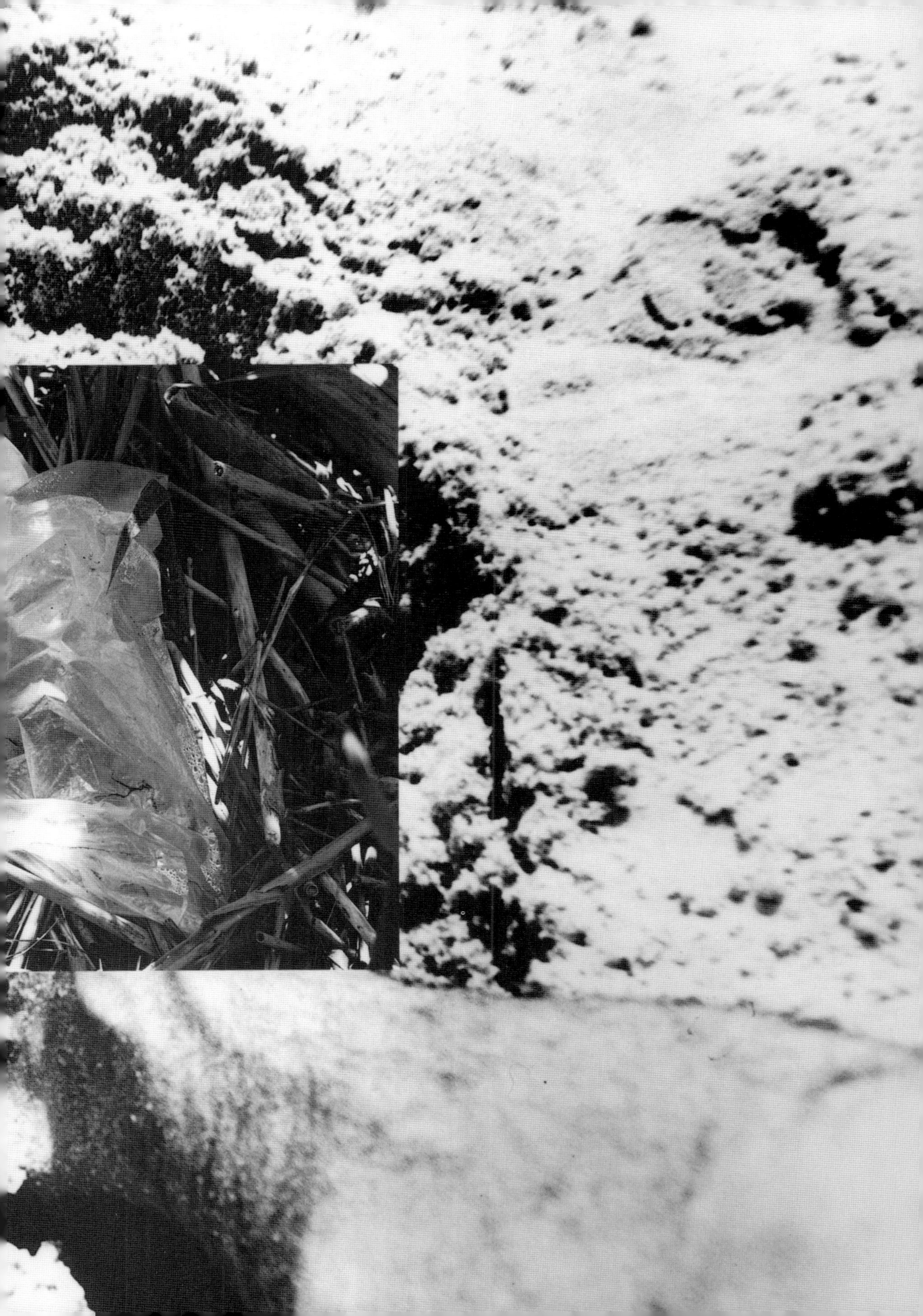

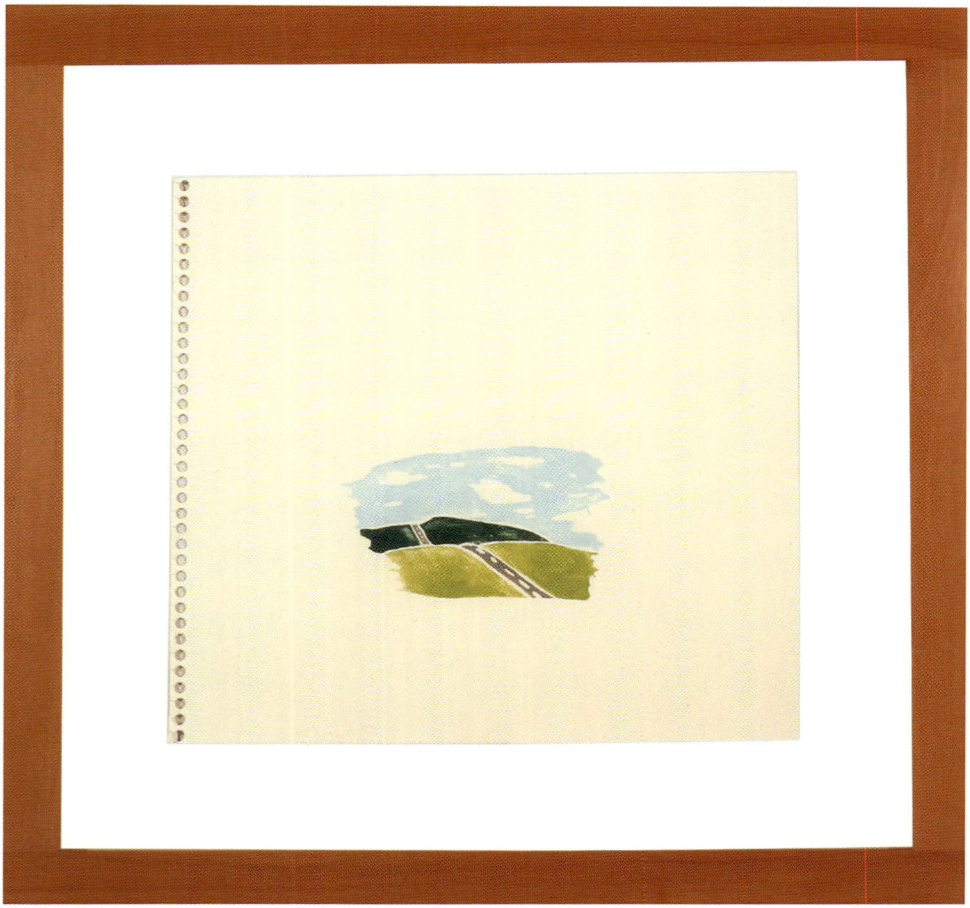

Untitled, 1979/2007

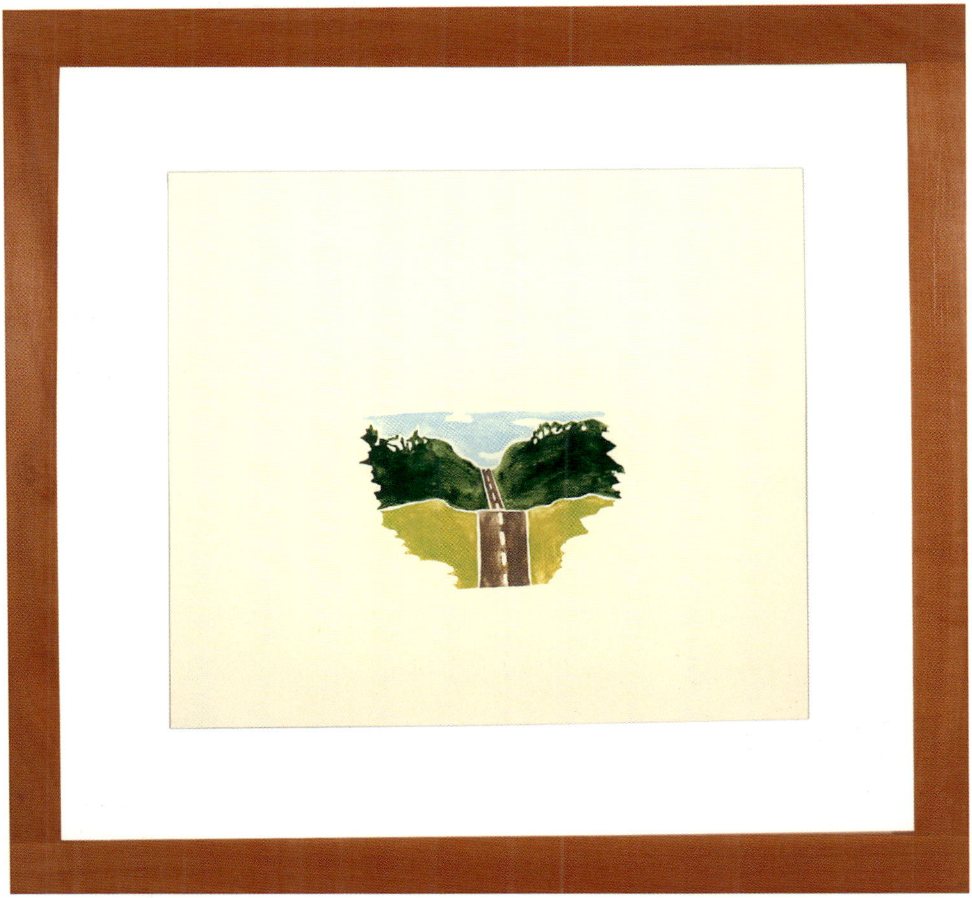

Highway, 1979/2007

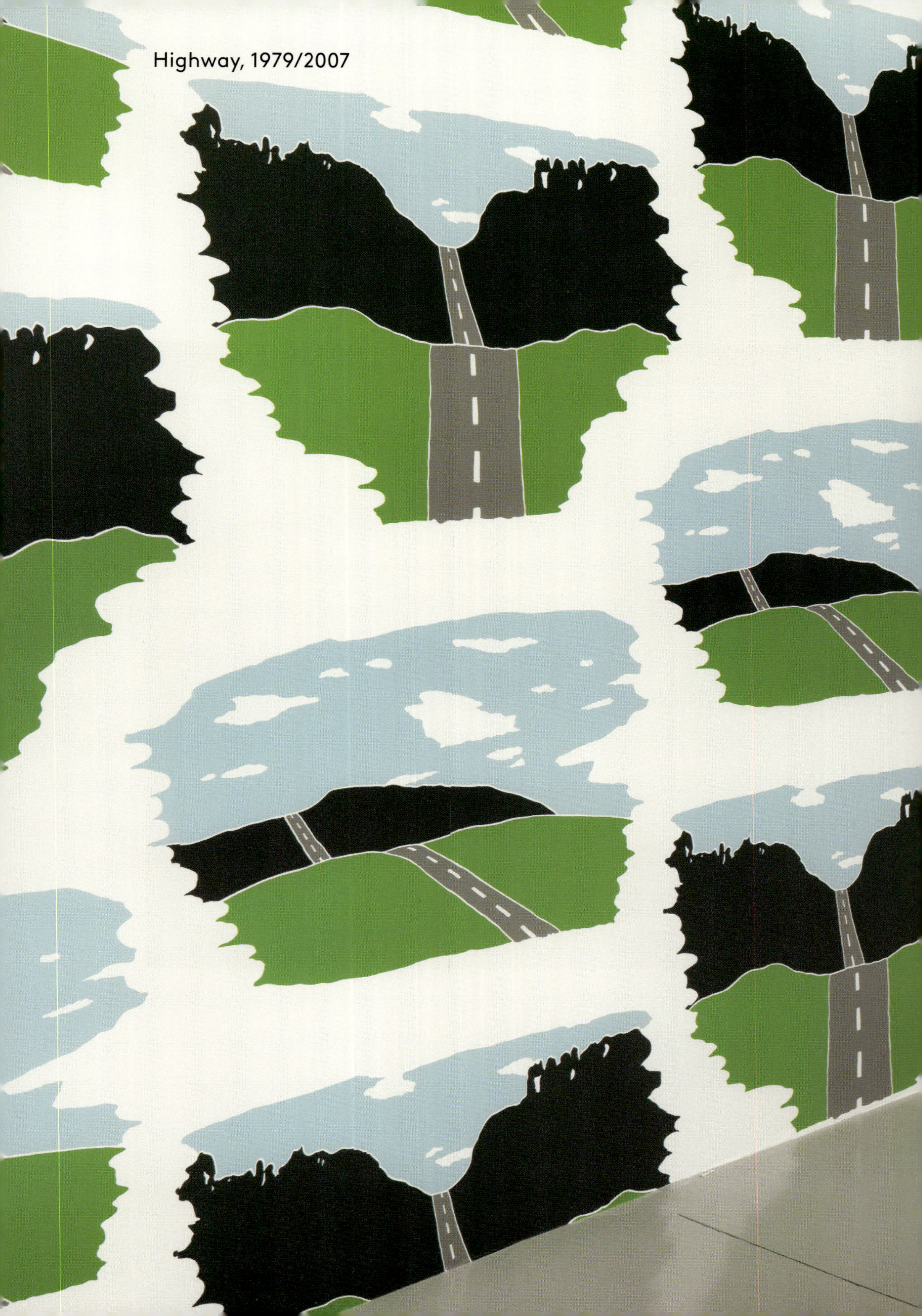

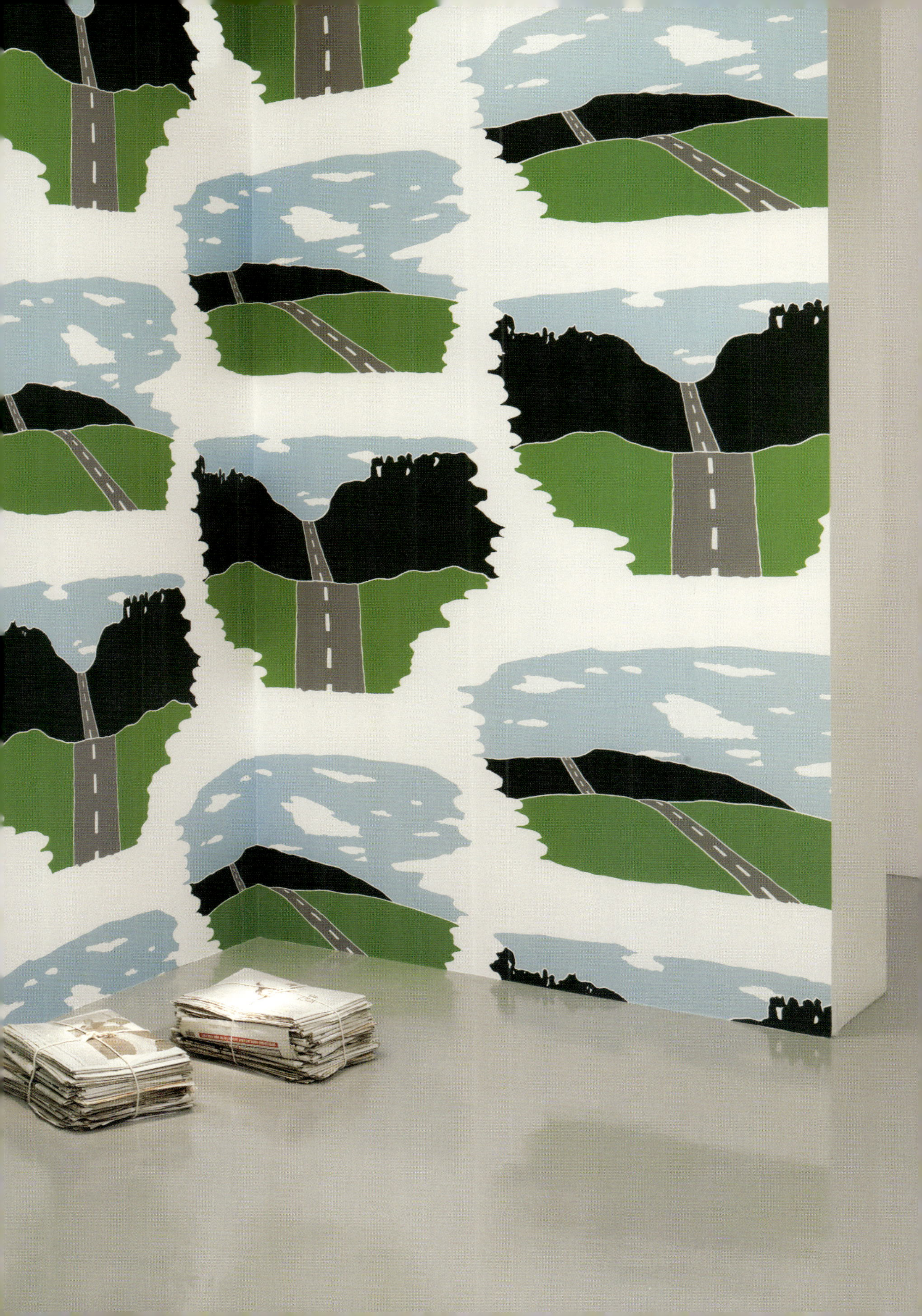

The Scary Sink, 1985

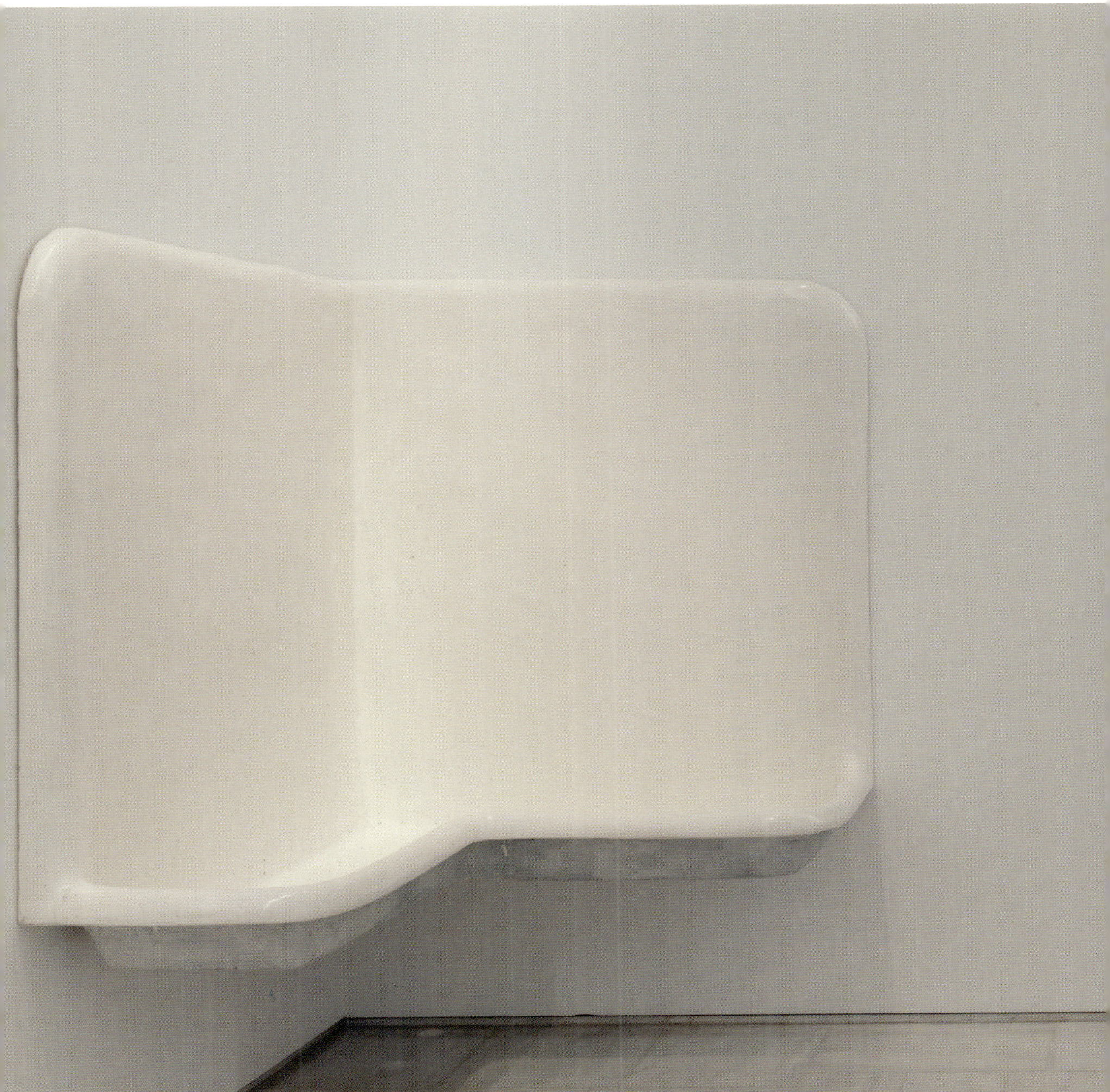

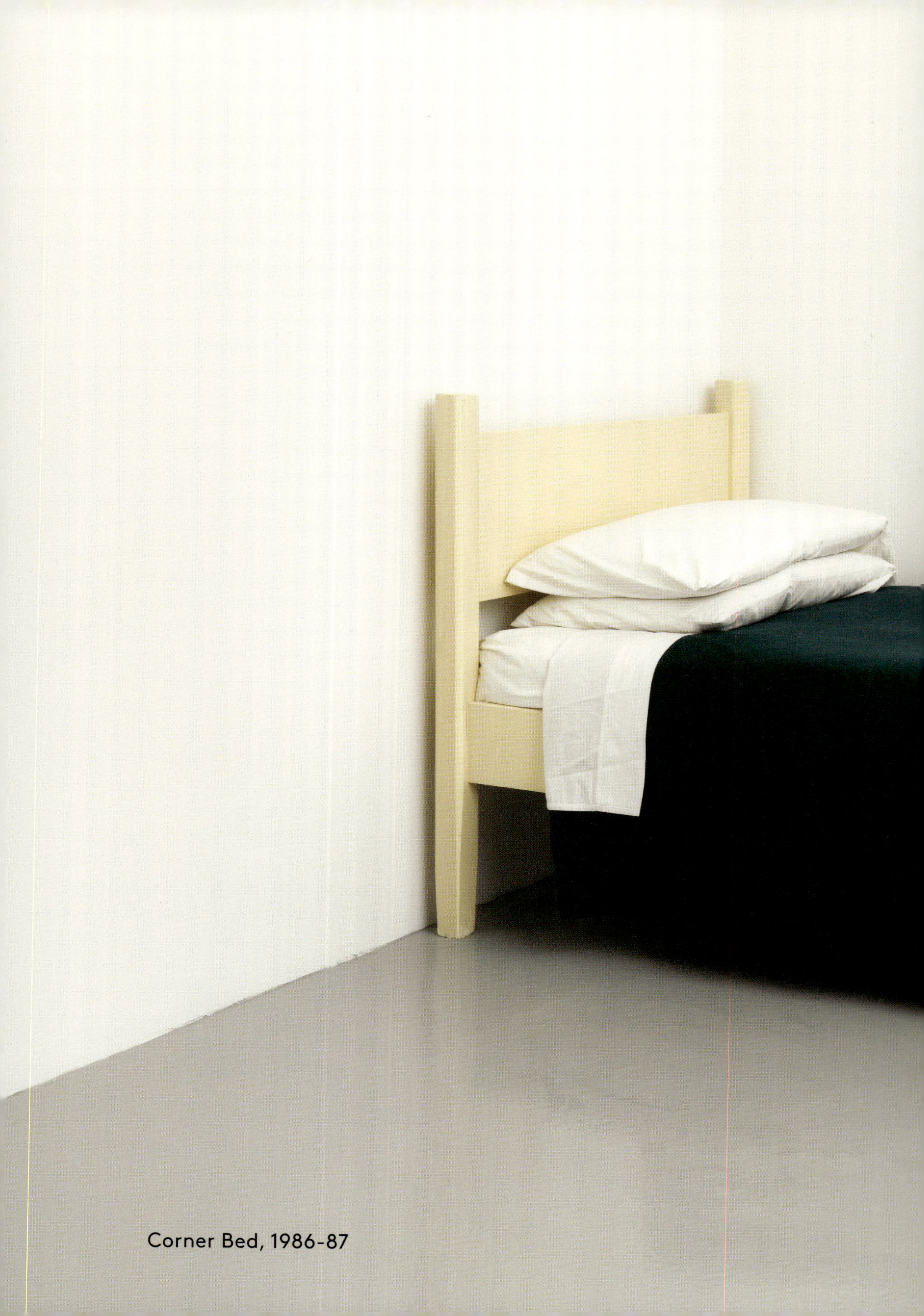

Corner Bed, 1986-87

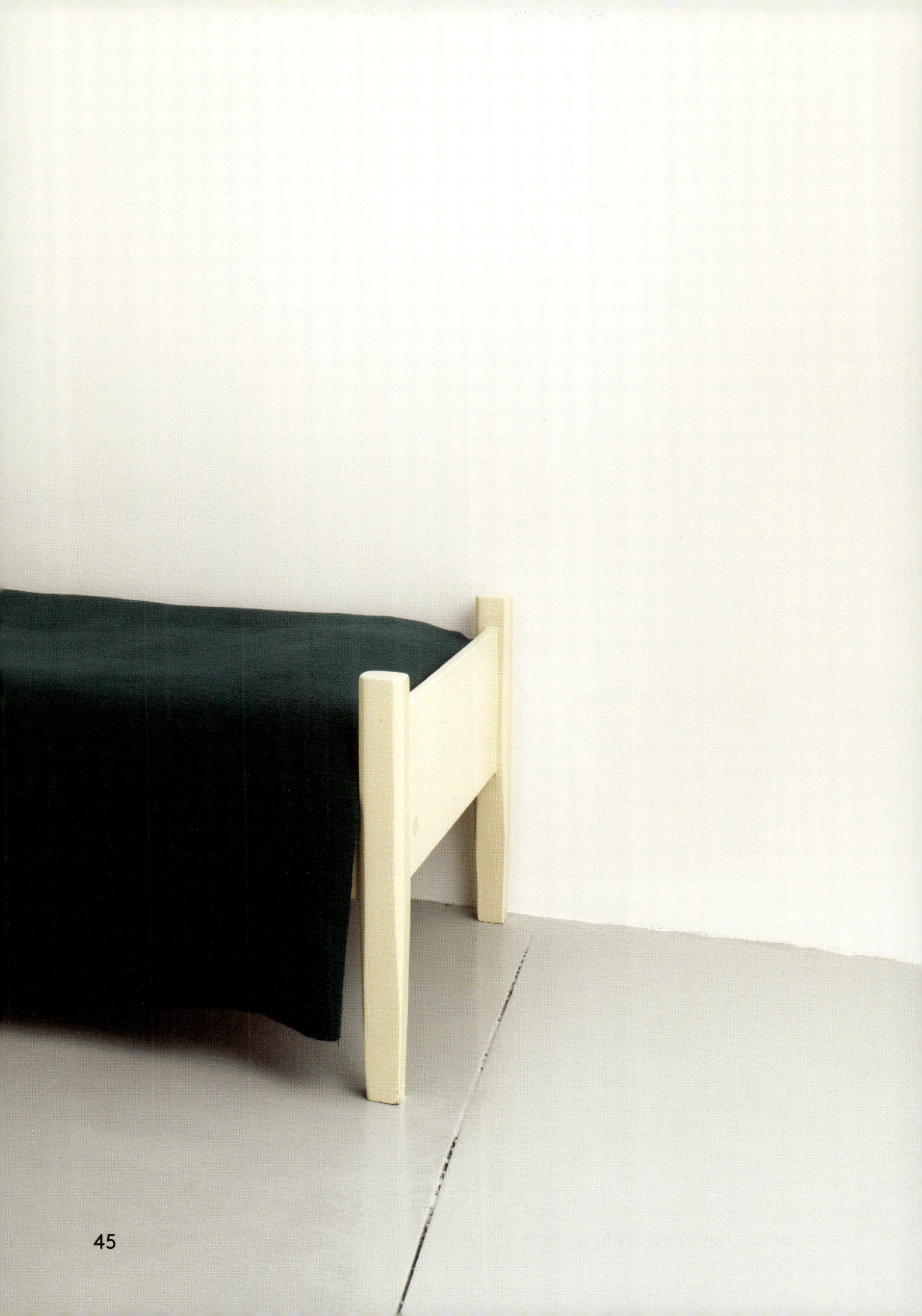

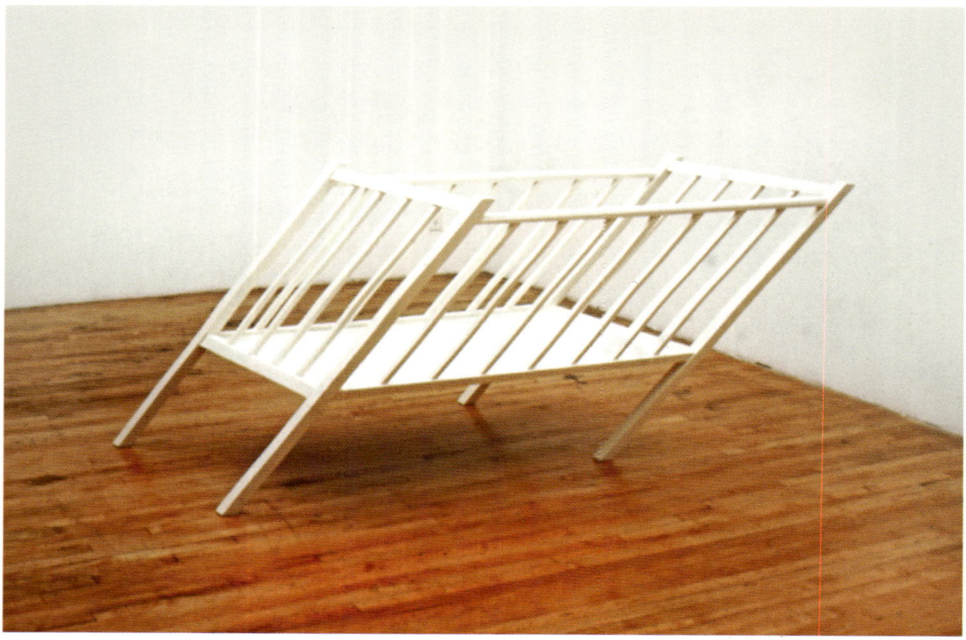

Pitched Crib, 1987

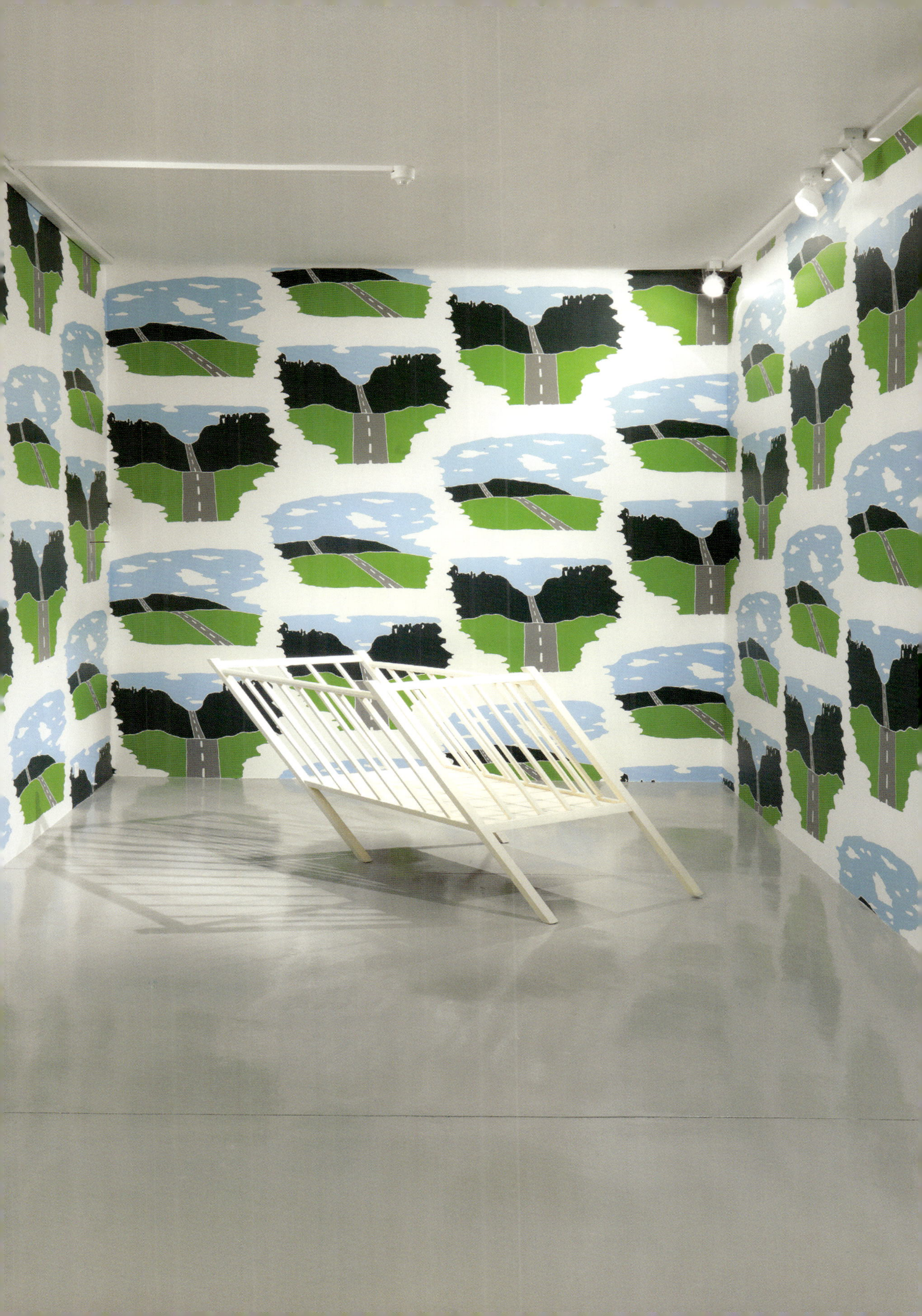

Untitled, 1989

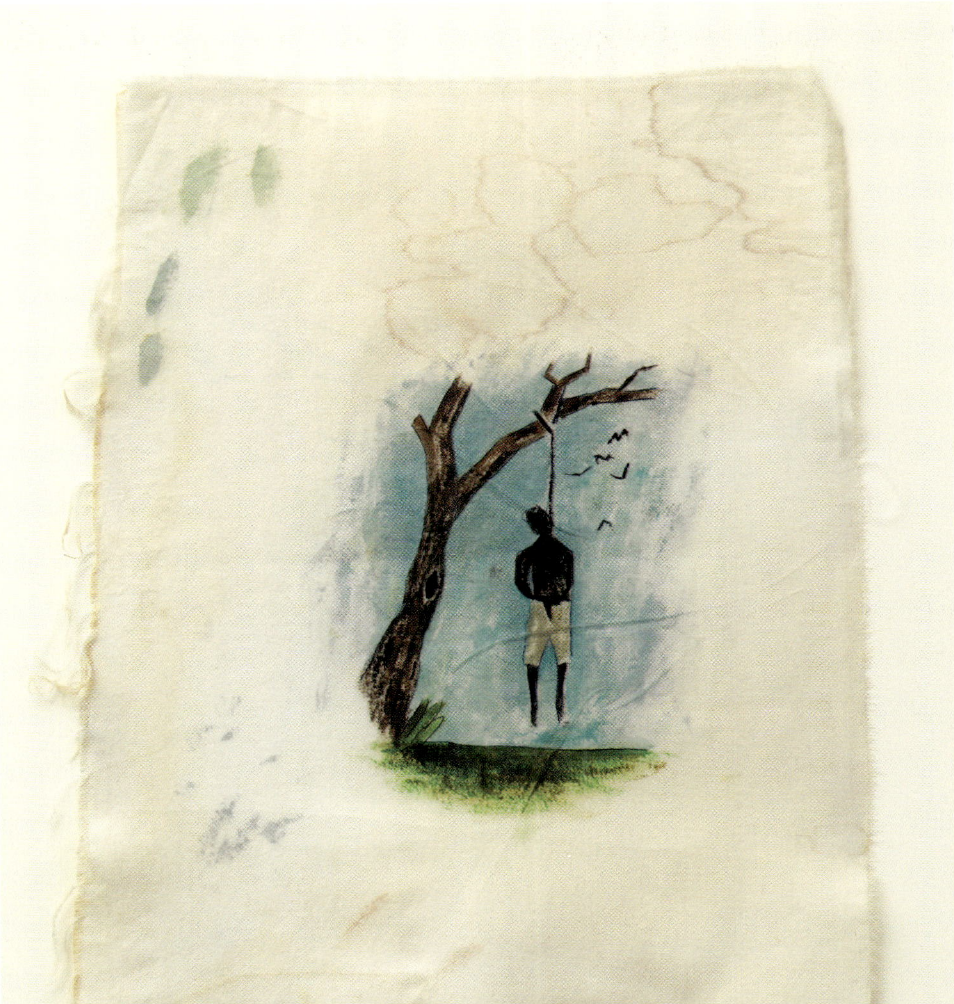

Two Breasts, 1990

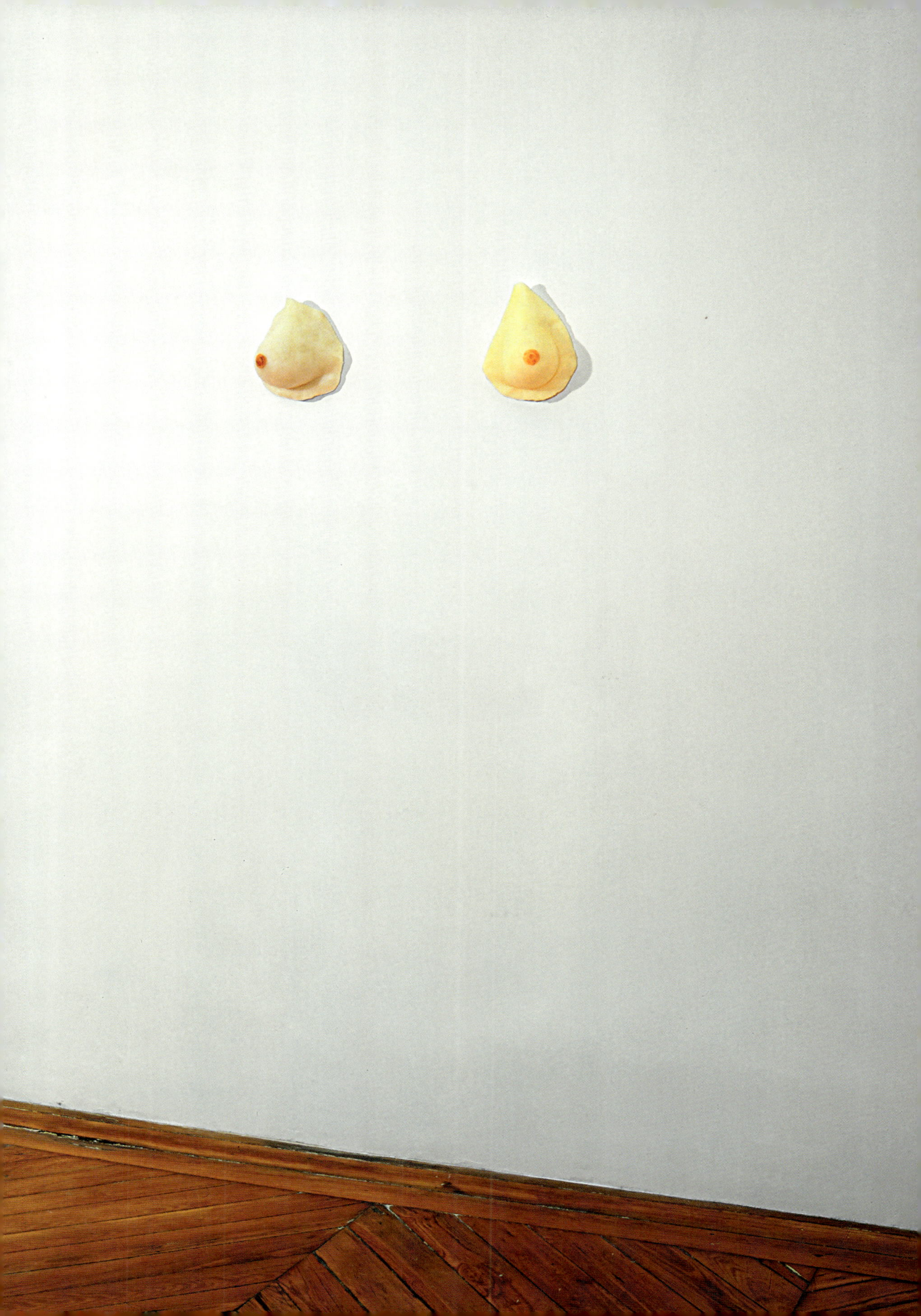

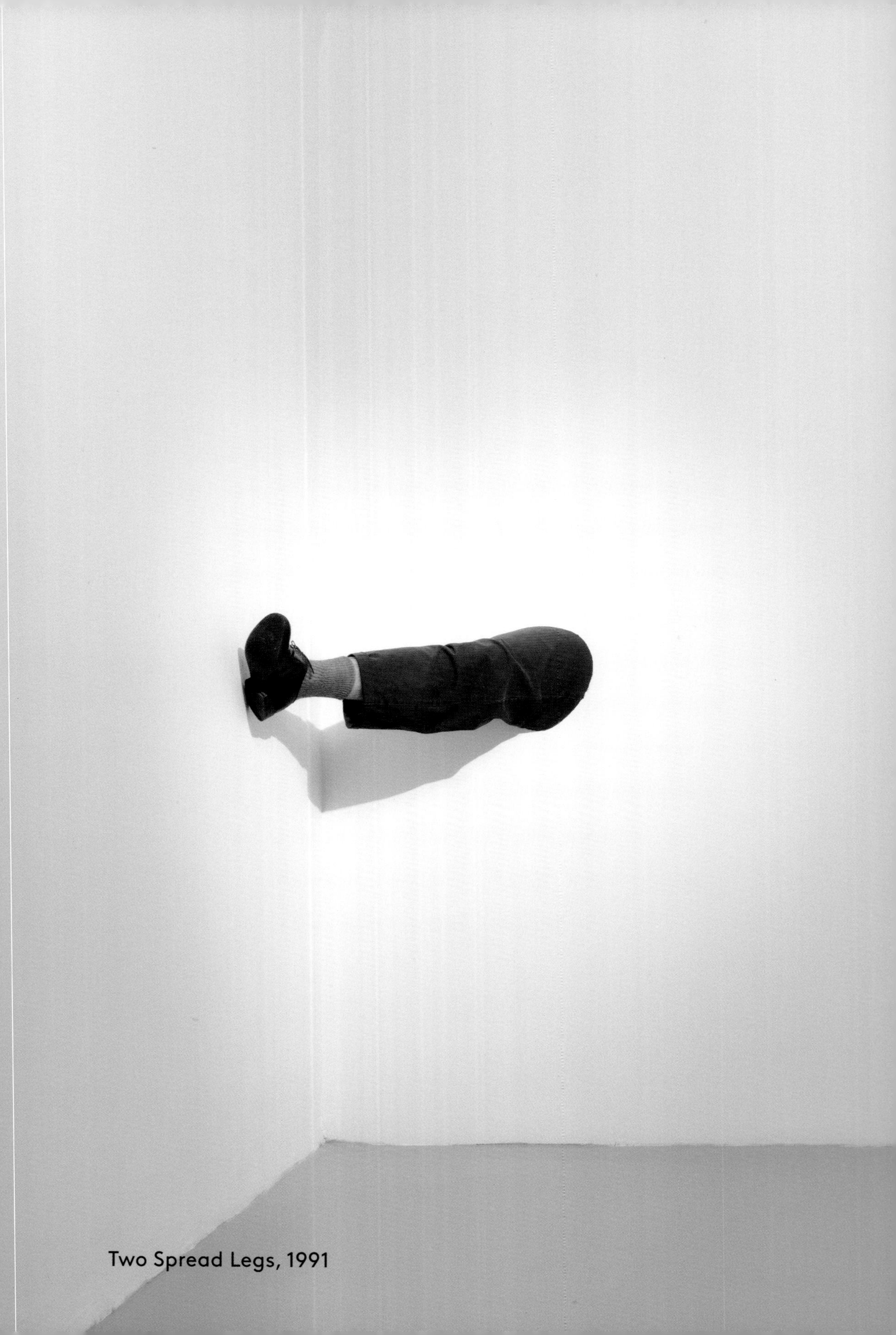

Two Spread Legs, 1991

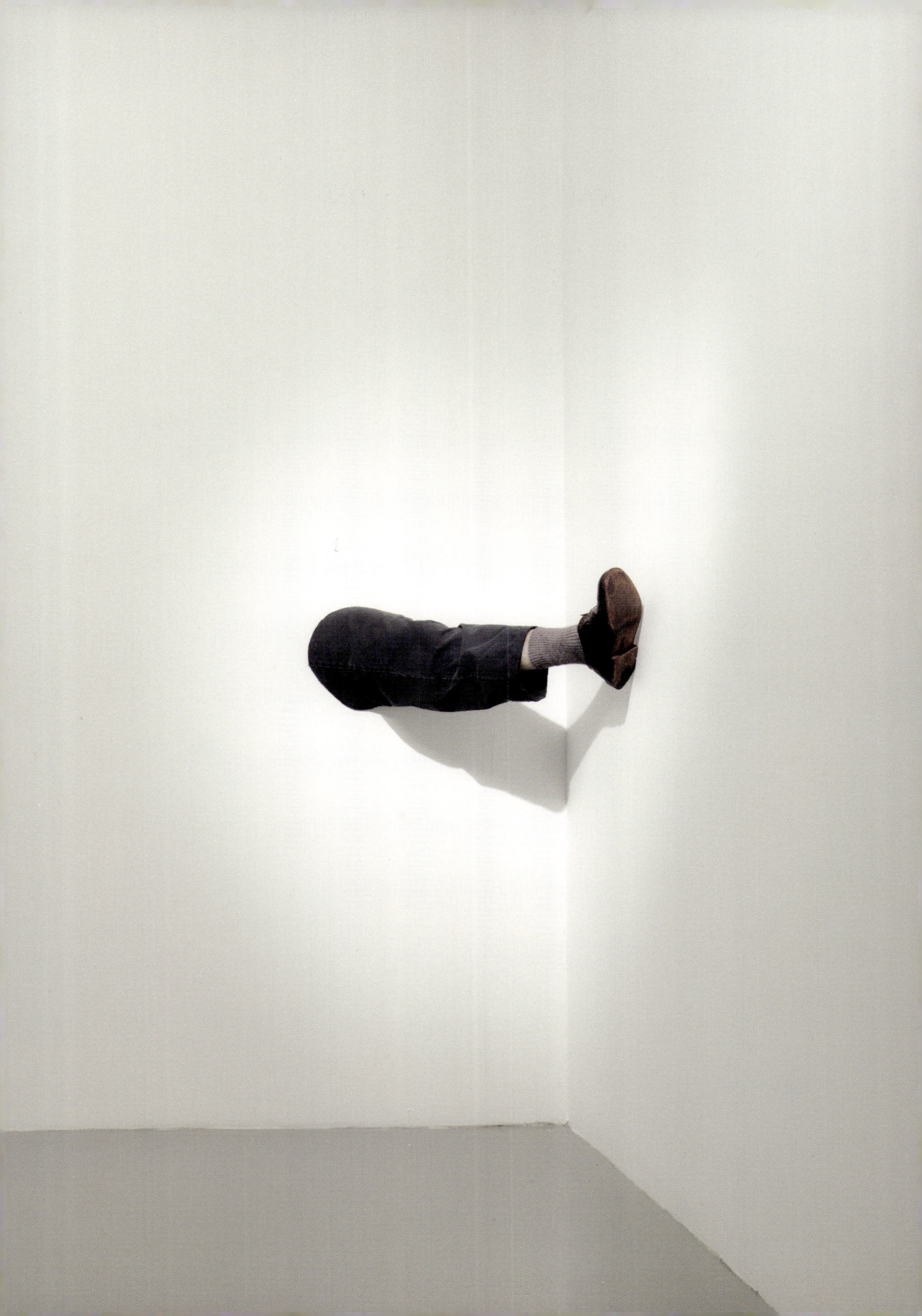

Newspaper, 1992

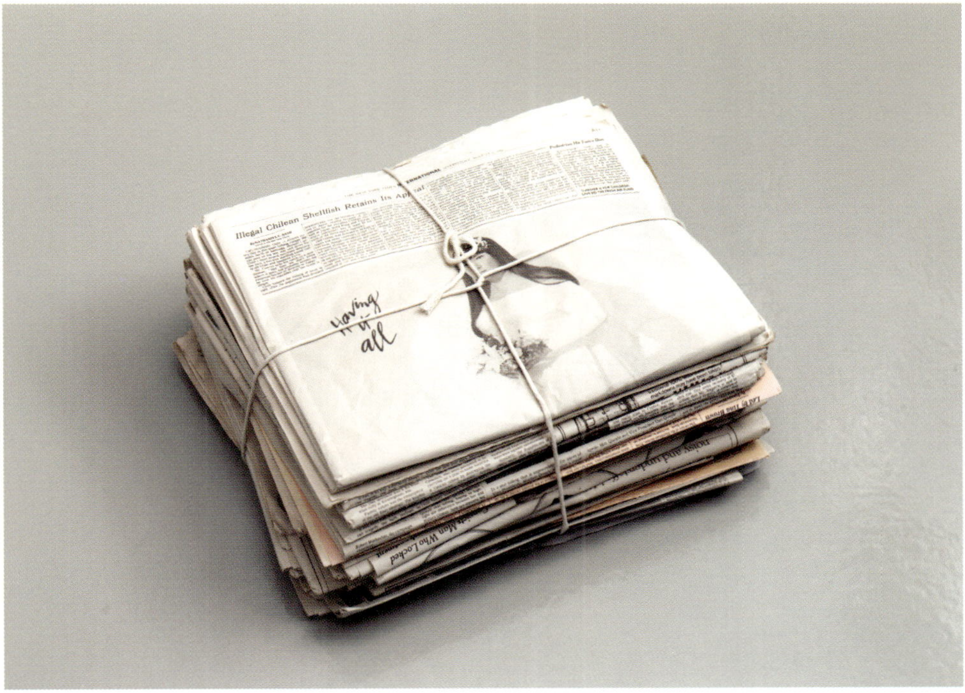
Illegal Chilean Shellfish Retains Its Appeal

Newspaper, 1992

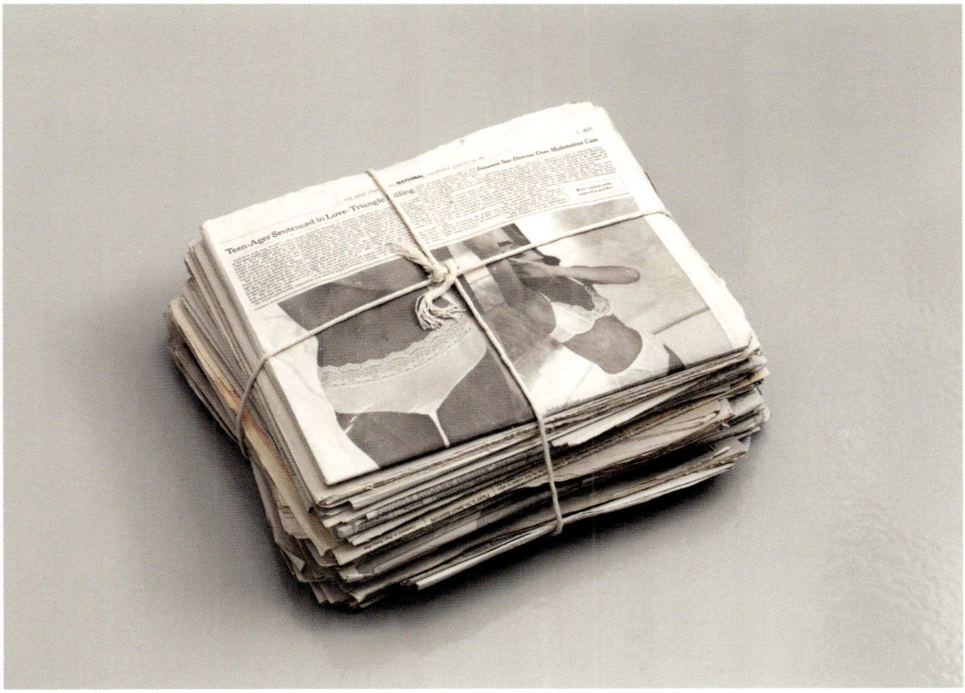
Teen-Ager Sentenced in Love-Triangle

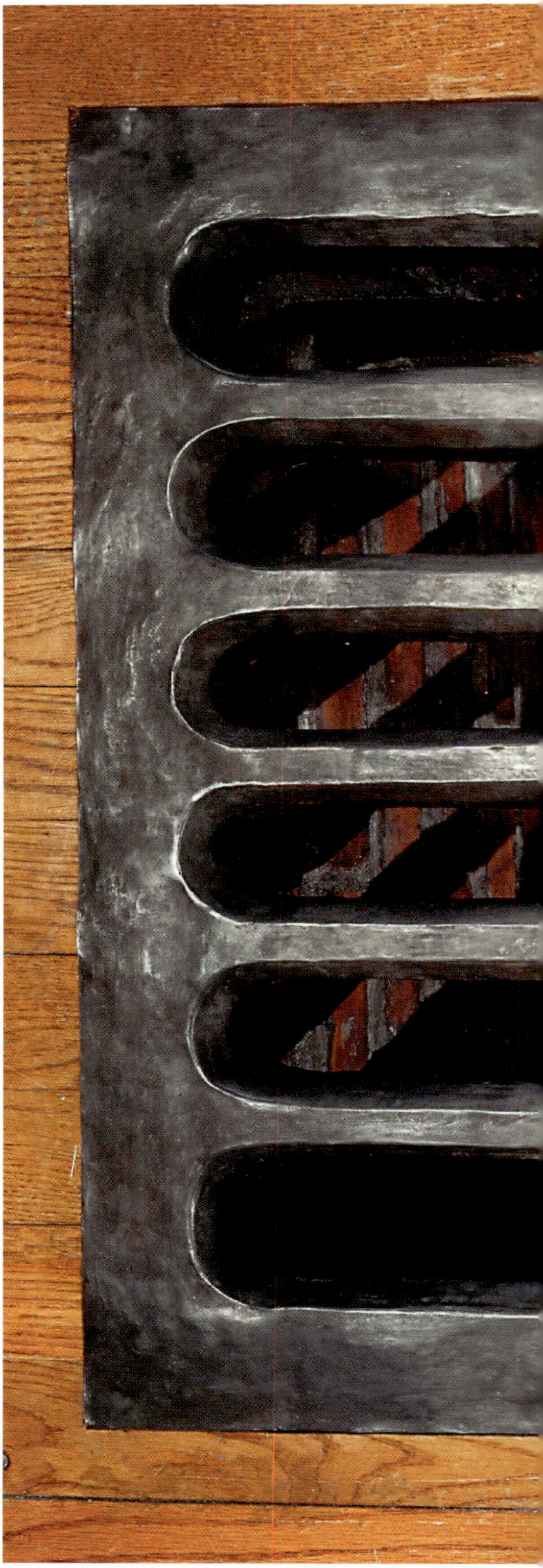

Untitled, 1993-94

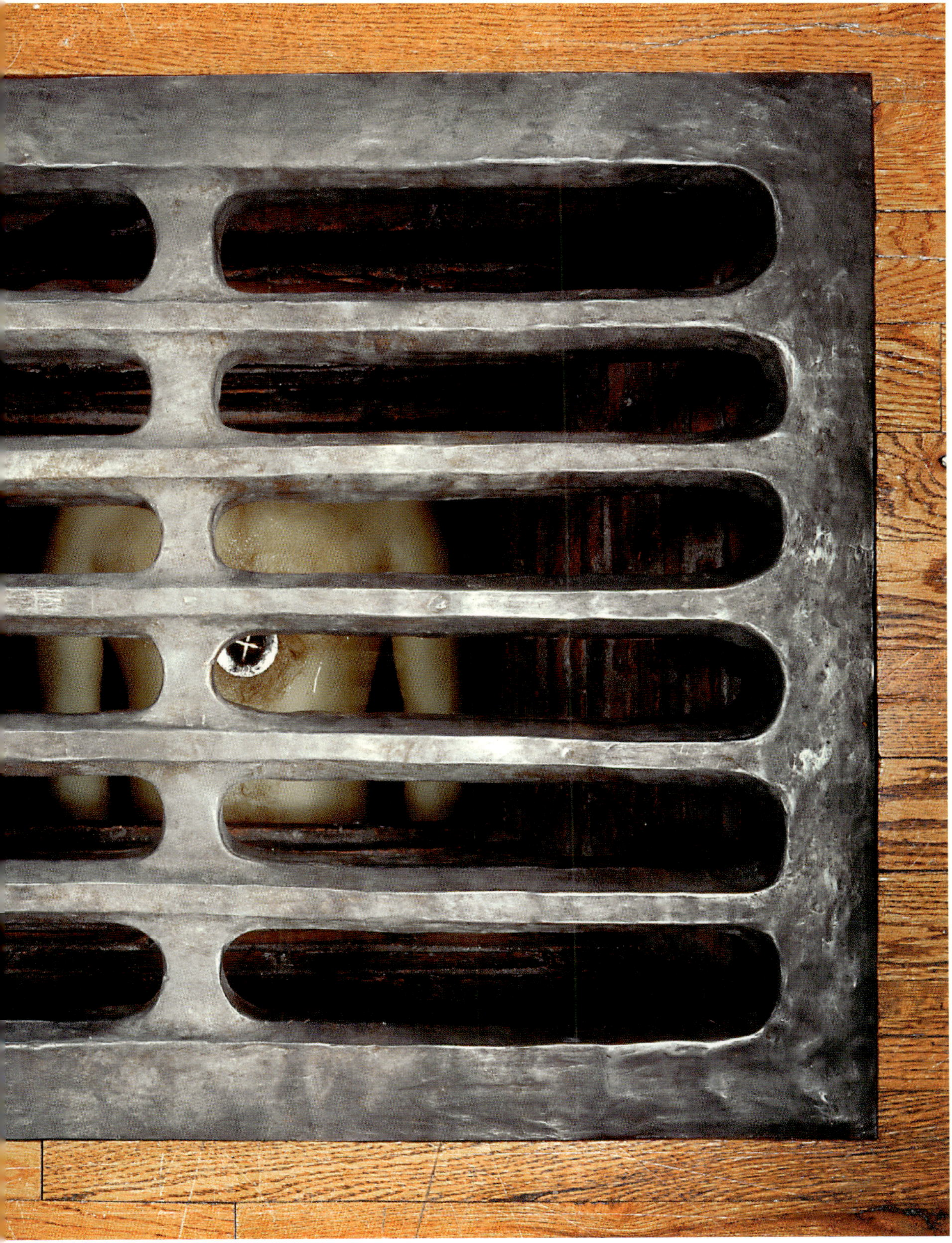

Untitled, 1993-94

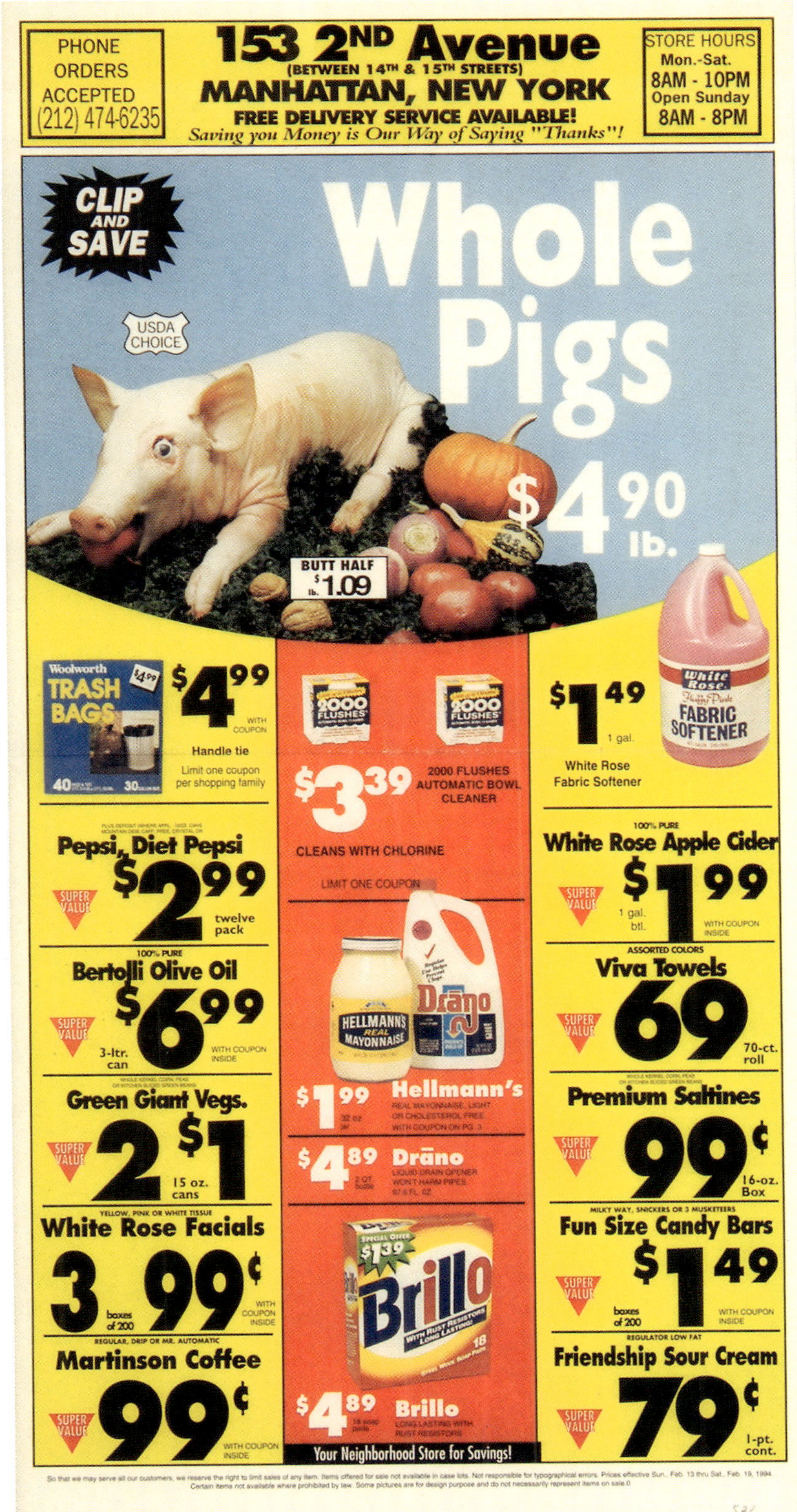

PHONE ORDERS ACCEPTED (212) 474-6235
153 2ND Avenue
(BETWEEN 14TH & 15TH STREETS)
MANHATTAN, NEW YORK
FREE DELIVERY SERVICE AVAILABLE!
Saving you Money is Our Way of Saying "Thanks"!
STORE HOURS Mon.-Sat. 8AM - 10PM Open Sunday 8AM - 8PM
CLIP AND SAVE
Whole Pigs
$4.90 lb.
USDA CHOICE
BUTT HALF $1.09 lb.
Woolworth TRASH BAGS
$4.99 WITH COUPON
Handle tie
Limit one coupon per shopping family
$3.39 2000 FLUSHES AUTOMATIC BOWL CLEANER
CLEANS WITH CHLORINE
LIMIT ONE COUPON
$1.49 1 gal.
White Rose Fabric Softener
White Rose FABRIC SOFTENER
Pepsi, Diet Pepsi
$2.99 twelve pack
SUPER VALUE
100% PURE
White Rose Apple Cider
$1.99 1 gal. btl. WITH COUPON INSIDE
100% PURE
Bertolli Olive Oil
$6.99 3-ltr. can WITH COUPON INSIDE
HELLMANN'S REAL MAYONNAISE
Drano
ASSORTED COLORS
Viva Towels
69 70-ct. roll
Green Giant Vegs.
2 $1 15 oz. cans
$1.99 Hellmann's
$4.89 Drāno
Premium Saltines
99¢ 16-oz. Box
YELLOW, PINK OR WHITE TISSUE
White Rose Facials
3 99¢ boxes of 200 WITH COUPON INSIDE
Brillo
MILKY WAY, SNICKERS OR 3 MUSKETEERS
Fun Size Candy Bars
$1.49 boxes of 200 WITH COUPON INSIDE
REGULAR, DRIP OR MR. AUTOMATIC
Martinson Coffee
99¢ WITH COUPON INSIDE
$4.89 Brillo
LONG LASTING WITH RUST RESISTORS
Your Neighborhood Store for Savings!
REGULATOR LOW FAT
Friendship Sour Cream
79¢ 1-pt. cont.
So that we may serve all our customers, we reserve the right to limit sales of any item. Items offered for sale not available in case lots. Not responsible for typographical errors. Prices effective Sun., Feb. 13 thru Sat., Feb. 19, 1994.
Certain items not available where prohibited by law. Some pictures are for design purpose and do not necessarily represent items on sale.0
R. Gober '93-4 52/75

Untitled, 1995

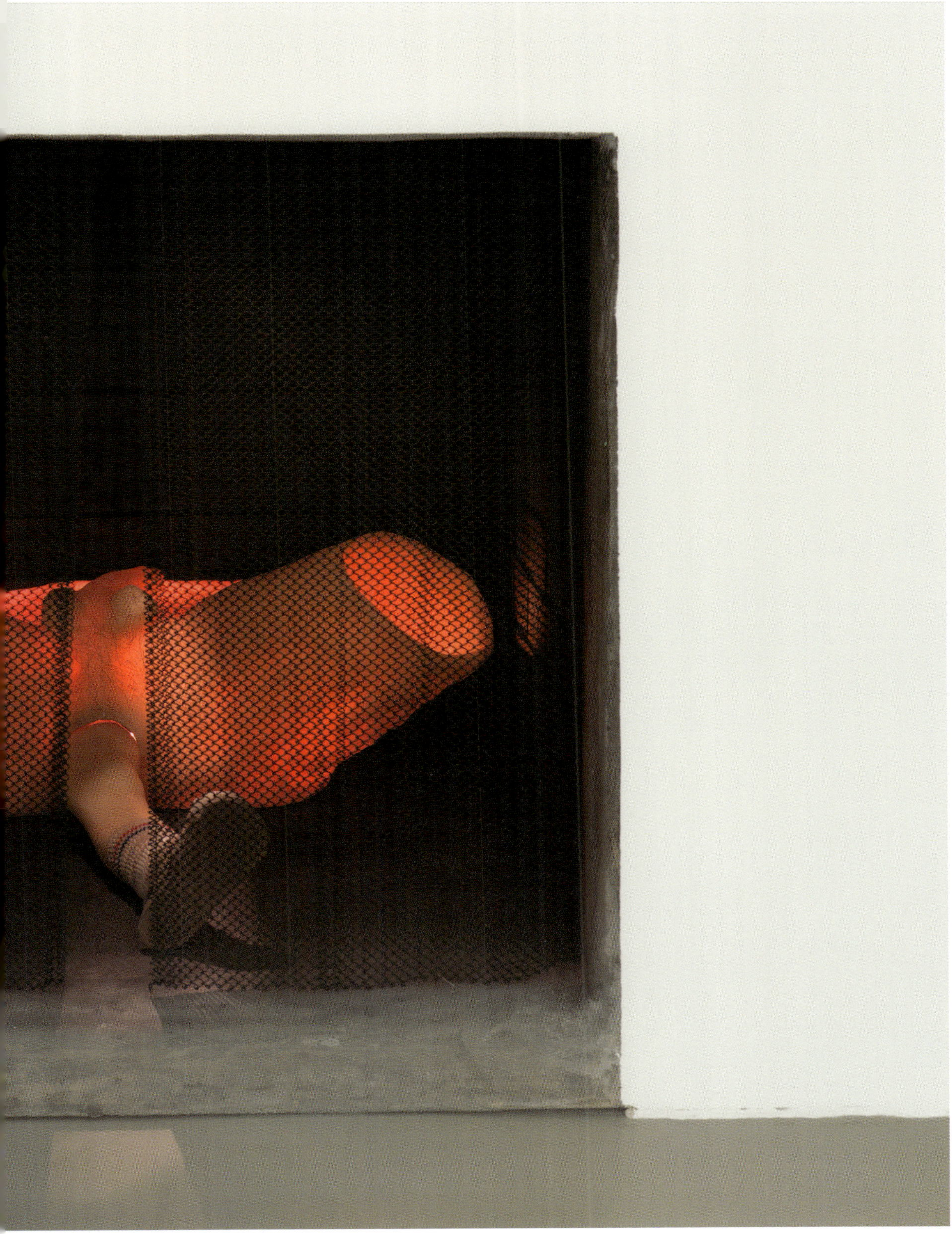

Untitled, 2000-2001

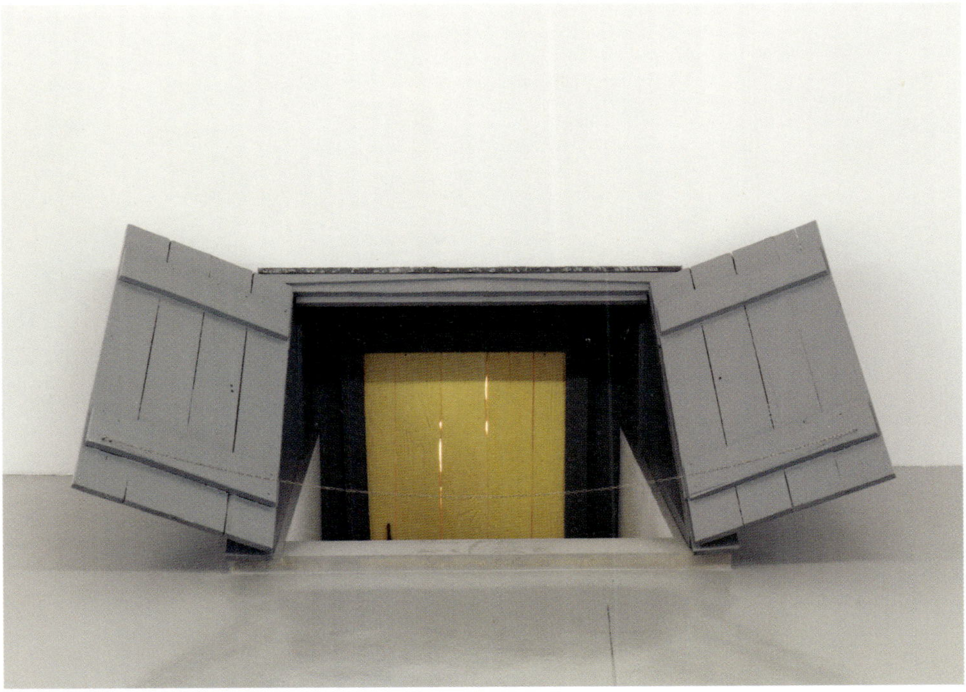

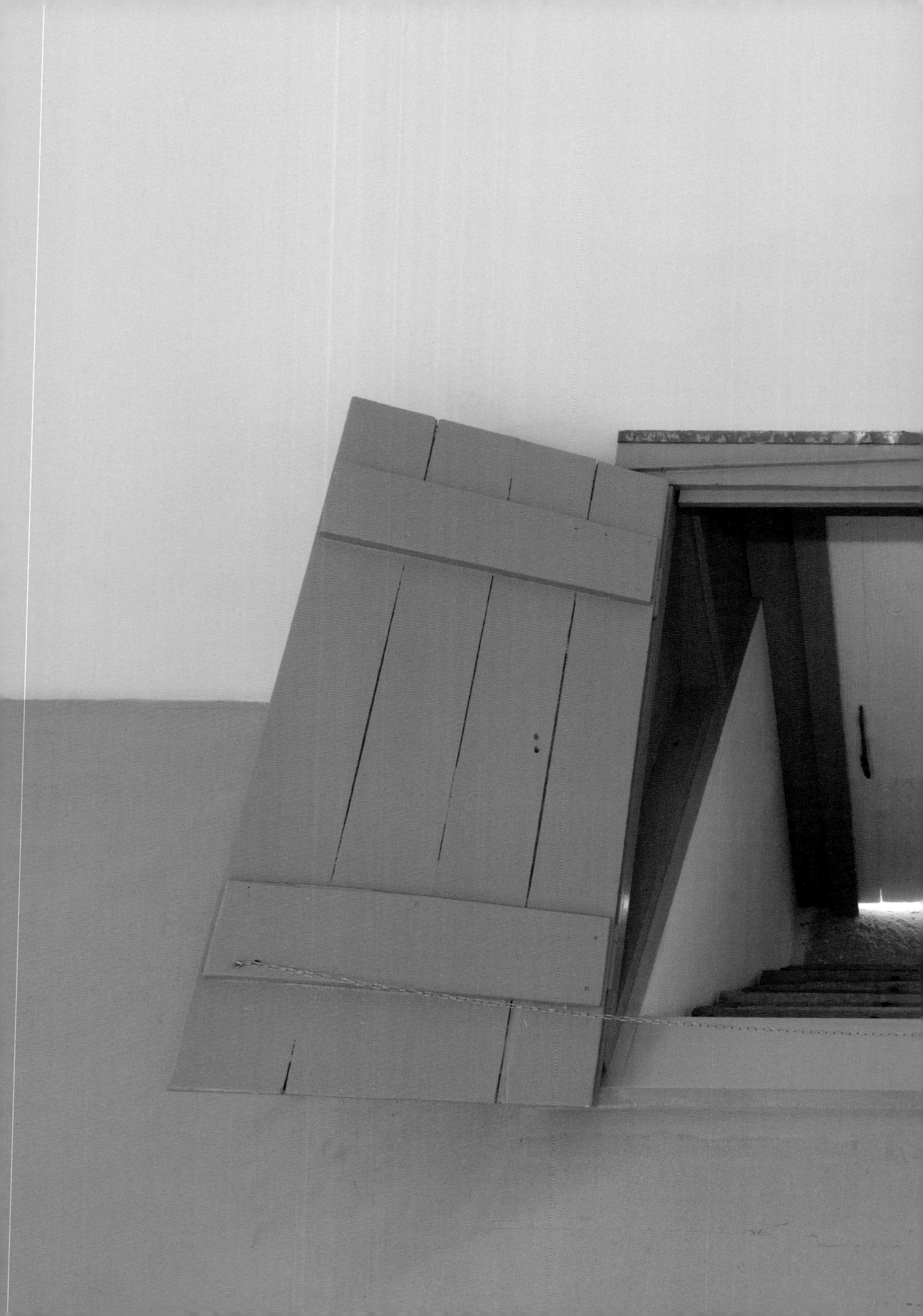

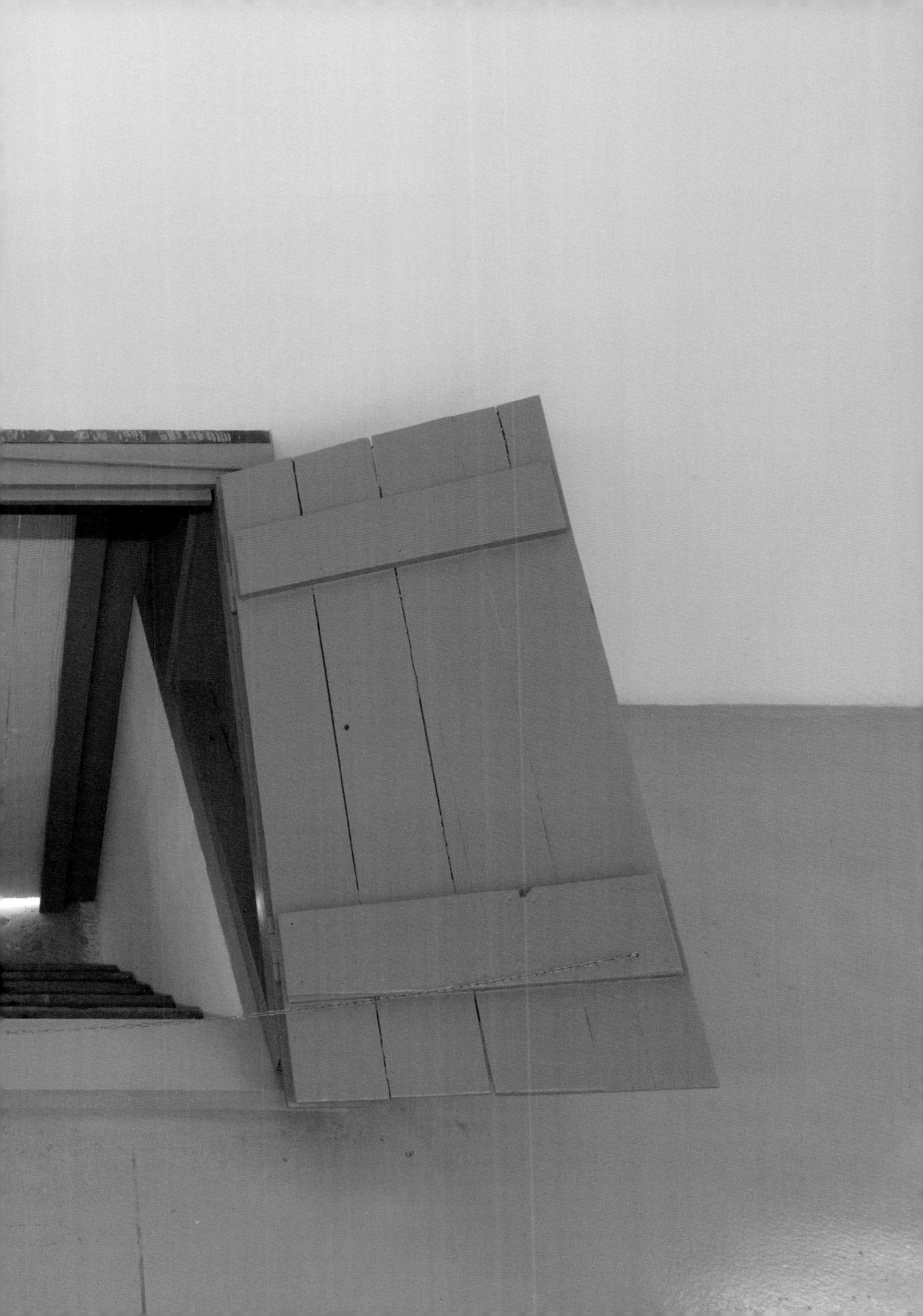

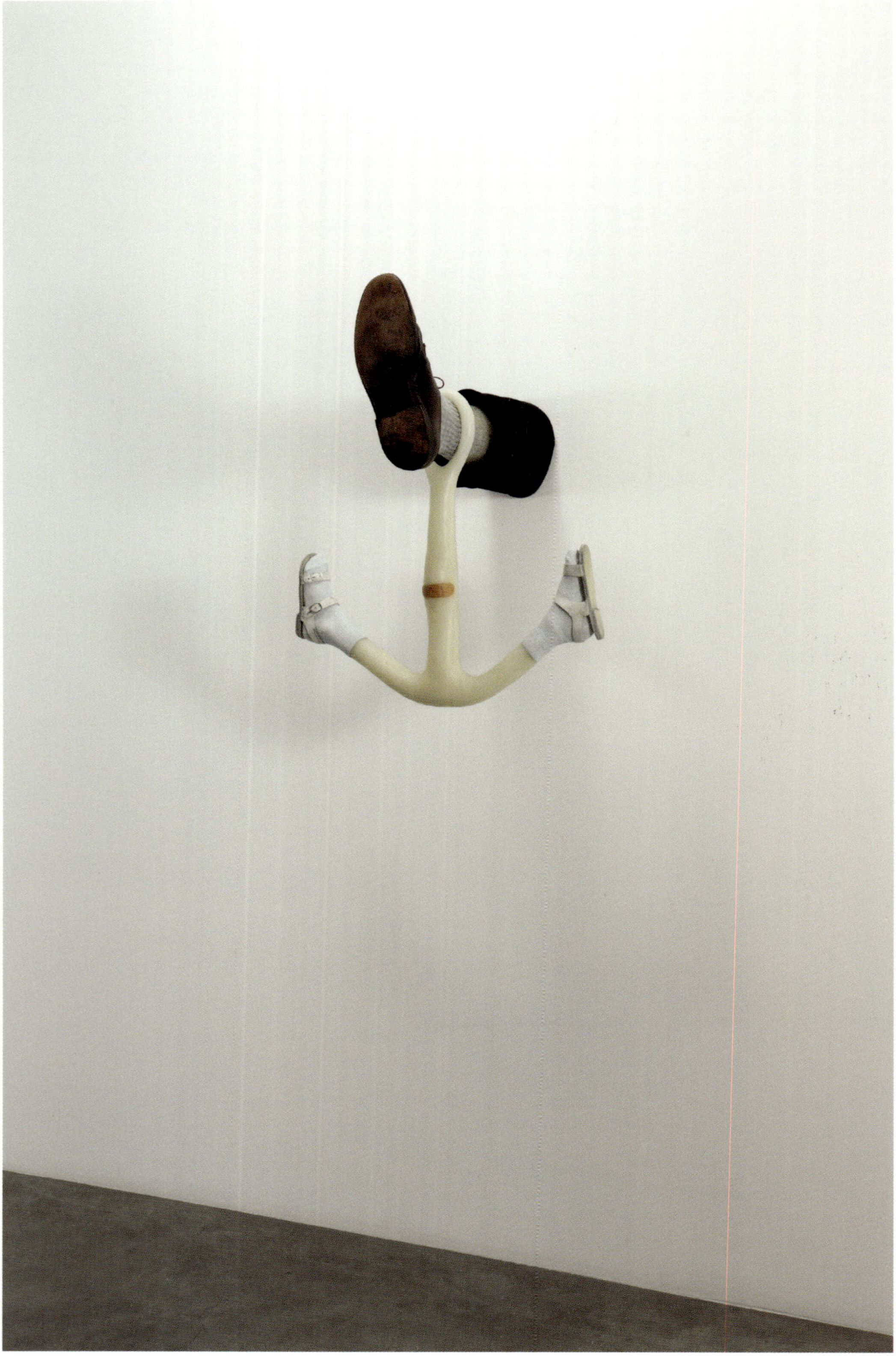

Untitled, 2008-9

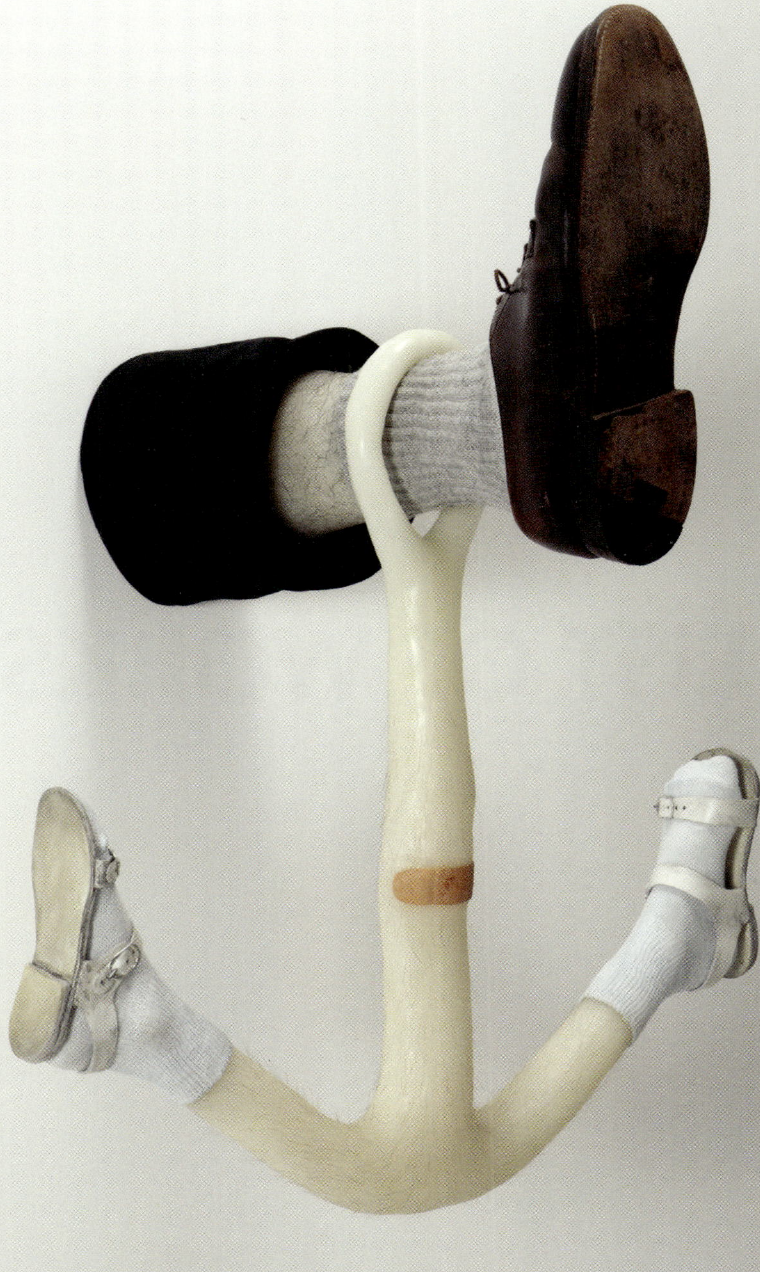

LIST OF WORKS

Dollhouse 4, 1978
Wood, paint, Plexiglas, corrugated cardboard, stones, cement, glue, and formica
69.8 x 119.3 x 55.8 cm

1978–2000, 1978–2000
Set of 22 silver gelatin prints
Each sheet: 65 x 88 cm; each image: 51 x 75 cm
Edition 3/5

Untitled, 1979/2007
Ink over linoleum block on paper
Two sheets, 22.9 x 26.4 cm each

Highway, 1979–2007
Hand-printed silkscreen on paper
Dimensions variable

The Scary Sink, 1985
Plaster, wood, steel, wire lath, and semi-gloss enamel paint
152.4 x 198.1 x 139.7 cm

Corner Bed, 1986–87
Wood, cotton, wool, and enamel paint
111 x 195 x 105 cm

Pitched Crib, 1987
Wood and enamel paint
97.2 x 195.6 x 132.1 cm

Untitled, 1989
Fabric paint on flannel
34.2 x 27.9 cm

Two Breasts, 1990
Beeswax and pigment
Left: 21 x 17.8 x 10 cm
Right: 18.5 x 17.8 x 10.5 cm

Two Spread Legs, 1991
Wood, beeswax, leather, cotton, human hair, and steel
Each leg: 27.9 x 88.9 x 69.8 cm

Newspaper, 1992
Photolithography on archival (Mohawk Super Fine) paper and twine
15.2 x 41.2 x 33.6 cm
Edition 2/10

Newspaper, 1992
Photolithography on archival (Mohawk Super Fine) paper and twine
15.2 x 40.6 x 35.6 cm
Edition 7/10

Untitled, 1993–94
Bronze, wood, brick, aluminum, beeswax, human hair, chrome-plated bronze, recycling pump, water, plaster, and latex paint
Bronze grate: 3.8 x 74.2 x 55.8 cm;
Box: 72.3 x 74.9 x 55.8 cm; Tank: 66 x 95.2 x 86.3 cm
Edition 1/2

Untitled, 1993–94
Photolithography on archival (French Dur-o-Tone) paper
66 x 39 cm, framed
Edition 52/75 + 10 AP

Untitled, 1995
Wood, beeswax, plaster, brick, leather, cotton, human hair, light bulbs, motor, and woven steel screen
101 x 119 x 117 cm (overall) x 76 cm (opening)

Untitled, 2000–2001
Wood, paint, concrete, cast plastic, and human hair
Overall approx. 203 x 122 x 183 cm

Untitled, 2008–9
Beeswax, cotton, leather, aluminum pull tabs, human hair, and oil paint
77 x 56 x 50 cm

ARTIST BIO

Robert Gober was born in Wallingford, Connecticut, in 1954. He first showed his work in 1984 and rapidly rose to prominence as one of the most significant artists of his generation. His work draws attention to the unnamable territory between reality and representation, concrete and abstract, expected and actual. Recognizable objects, laboriously recreated, assume additional, alternative implications.

His recent solo exhibitions include *The Heart Is Not a Metaphor* at the Museum of Modern Art, New York (2014); *Sculpture Drawings Studies* at the Matthew Marks Gallery, Los Angeles (2013); *Works from the Emanuel Hoffmann Foundation and the Öffentlichen Kunstsammlung Basel* at the Museum für Gegenwartskunst, Basel (2012); *Sculptures and Installations 1979–2007* at the Schaulager, Basel (2007); and the United States Pavilion at the 49th Venice Biennale (2001), among many others. He has been featured in numerous group exhibitions, including *Take It or Leave It: Institution, Image, Ideology* at the Hammer Museum, Los Angeles (2014); *The System of Objects* (2013), *Alpha Omega* (2010), *A Guest + A Host = A Ghost* (2009), and *Fractured Figure* (2008) at the DESTE Foundation for Contemporary Art, Athens; *Regarding Warhol: Sixty Artists, Fifty Years* at the Metropolitan Museum of Art, New York (2012); *Radical Conceptual* at the Museum für Moderne Kunst, Frankfurt (2010); *Skin Fruit* at the New Museum, New York (2010); *Collecting Collections* at the Museum of Contemporary Art, Los Angeles (2008); and *Dream & Trauma* at the Kunsthalle Wien and MUMOK, Vienna (2007). Robert Gober lives and works in New York.

AUTHOR BIO

Johanna Burton is director and curator of education at the New Museum in New York. An art historian, critic, and curator, she is considered a leading scholar of contemporary art. Her articles and reviews have appeared in numerous journals and publications, including *Artforum*, *Art Journal*, *October*, and *Texte zur Kunst*, as well as in exhibition catalogues for institutions throughout the world.

Burton has curated or co-curated a number of exhibitions, including *Anti-Establishment* at the Center for Curatorial Studies at Bard College (2012) and *Take It or Leave It: Institution, Image, Ideology* at the Hammer Museum in Los Angeles (2014), which featured Robert Gober's work.

Prior to her work at the New Museum, Burton served as the director of curatorial studies in the masters program at Bard College, and associate director and senior faculty member of the Whitney Museum of American Art's Independent Study Program. Burton has earned graduate degrees from the State University of New York at Stony Brook, New York University, and Princeton University.

I first met Bob in the mid-eighties during the excitement of New York's East Village art scene. He very quickly became one of the artists that I began to collect. To this day I am still amazed at his aplomb during the opening of his 2007 show at the Schaulager when he stood in front of the crowd that had gathered to hear him speak and said: "I'm Robert Gober. You can ask me anything you want." My heartfelt thanks to him, and to Johanna Burton, who perfectly articulates his enigmatic take on our familiar world, and to Massimiliano Gioni, who has commissioned all of the essays in the series. Special thanks to Karen Marta and Sue Medlicott for their unwavering enthusiasm, and to Brendan Dugan, whose design has established the unmistakable visual identity of the *2000 Words* series.

—Dakis Joannou

Robert Gober
2000 Words

Commissioning Editor: Massimiliano Gioni
Editor: Karen Marta
Design: An Art Service
Project Managers: Regina Alivisatos, Dustin Cosentino
Registrar: Natasha Polymeropoulos
Copy Editor: Miles Champion
Production: The Production Department

Published by:
The DESTE Foundation for Contemporary Art
Filellinon 11 & Em. Pappa St.
N. Ionia 142 34, Athens
www.deste.gr

Cover: Robert Gober, *Dollhouse 4*, 1978
Special thanks to Claudia Carson at Robert Gober Studio

Distributed in the Americas by:
ARTBOOK | D.A.P.
155 Sixth Avenue, 2nd Floor
New York, NY 10013
www.artbook.com

Distributed in Europe by:
Buchhandlung Walther König
Ehrenstrasse 4
50672 Köln
www.buchhandlung-walther-koenig.de

Printed in Greece by Alta Grafico S.A. Printing and Graphic Arts

ISBN: 978-618-5039-14-1